VOCABULARY FOR ADULTS

JACK S. ROMINE
Merritt College
Oakland, California

JOHN WILEY & SONS
New York • Chichester • Brisbane • Toronto

Editors: Judy Wilson and Irene Brownstone
Production Manager: Ken Burke
Editorial Supervisor: Winn Kalmon
Artist: Martha Hairston
Composition and Make-up: Frank Propellor

Library of Congress Cataloging in Publication Data

Romine, Jack S.
    Vocabulary for adults.

    (Wiley self-teaching guides)
    1. Vocabulary. 2. English language—Foreign elements—
Greek. 3. English language—Foreign elements—Latin I. Title
PE1449.R67   422'.4'8   75-17660
ISBN 0-471-73285-0

Printed in the United States of America

10 9 8 7 6 5

VOCABULARY FOR ADULTS

To the Reader

If you were interested enough to pick up this book and look it over, your command of vocabulary is obviously less than you would like it to be. This book can make no claim to magic, but it can be a valuable tool to help you expand your vocabulary. First, you must realize that all of us have two different kinds of vocabulary. At the core of our everyday conversation we use native English or Anglo-Saxon words like father, mother, earth, sun, sky, moon, cow, fire, water, go, and pray. These short words tend to be informal and nonacademic, and they seldom if ever cause any difficulty. Most of them were acquired before we ever left grade school. The troublesome words come from the second kind of vocabulary; they tend to be formal and we use them more in writing than in speaking. In short, they are the academic words. We call them academic because they have been borrowed chiefly from Latin and Greek and are associated with the sciences, the humanities, and other areas of learning. Examples are dysfunction, metamorphic, empathy, and syllogism.

This book concentrates on academic words, the so-called "big words." They do not have to be memorized or learned separately. There is a shortcut. Using the word-part approach, you can rapidly expand your ability to use and understand these words—even if you've never seen them before. Take, for example, the Latin word element cur, meaning "run." If you swim against the current, you swim against "running" water. If you suffer from a recurrent illness, the illness keeps "running back" or happening again and again. An excursion into the countryside is a "running outside" of the area where you live; the incursions of enemy forces would mean their "running into" (attacking) territory that is not their own. If you quickly scan or "run through" an essay, we say you gave the essay a cursory reading, often implying haste or carelessness. A public utilities official warns that a local two-hour blackout is the precursor of widespread power failures. He means that the blackout is something that "runs before" and signals the approach of something else, in this case widespread power failures. Cour is a variant of cur; thus, a diplomatic courier is a "runner" of messages between governments.

The goal of this book is to help you learn the major Greek and Latin word parts that form so many important English words. Once you catch on to the basic meaning of word parts such as the root cur (cour) and the prefixes ex and in, you will begin to absorb new words in groups rather than one at a time—a much more efficient method than memorizing single words. This word-part approach is possible because so many thousands of words in English are combinations of small words borrowed from Latin and Greek.

You will also learn how to cope with new words at the time you encounter them. Knowledge of word parts offers a good way of determining the meaning of an unfamiliar word—and it is the method you will be practicing throughout this book. Suppose you heard someone say, "The doctor prescribed diathermy to relieve the pain in Joe's back." If you did not already know the meaning of diathermy, you could only tell (from the context) that diathermy is some kind of treatment for relieving pain. If, however, you knew that the root therm means "heat," you would know that the treatment is based on the use of heat. If in addition you knew that the prefix dia meant "through," you could quickly translate the literal meaning "heat through" into "a method of relieving pain by sending heat through the body." Thus, at the time you first encountered the word, you would have figured out enough of its probable meaning to understand the sentence.

In many cases the literal meaning of a word is practically all you need to master it. Democracy, for example, literally means "people rule or government," and a thermometer is "that which measures heat." However, language is alive, growing, and slowly changing over the years. Some words have acquired later or changed meanings. Originally symposium simply meant "drinking together," but now we use it to mean a gathering held for the purpose of exchanging ideas, especially on a particular topic. Think about it for a moment and you will see a bridge between the literal meaning and the current meaning. Obviously drinking together normally involves a discussion; now the word stands for the discussion itself. (A good deal of drinking still accompanies some of the symposiums I have attended.) So although knowing the literal meaning of a word is valuable, you must also become sensitive to context clues and you must occasionally rely on a precise dictionary definition.

Although the language is complex, subtle, and ever-changing, a knowledge of the basic words in this book will help you use and understand vocabulary—both new and old—more effectively in your everyday life.

Oakland, California
August, 1975

Jack S. Romine

How to Use This Book

Vocabulary for Adults is designed to help you expand your vocabulary by learning to use and interpret the major Greek and Latin word parts appearing in many English words.

Using this Guide's special self-teaching format, you will be applying what you learn about word parts throughout the book, as you use and interpret new vocabulary. This book is organized very simply. Chapter 1 introduces the word parts—the roots, prefixes, and suffixes—and shows how they combine to form so many words in English. Chapters 2 through 6 are divided into numbered units, each of which focuses on a specific Greek or Latin word part, and presents some words, or derivatives, it forms with other word parts. In each unit, you will have a chance to work with the new words and word parts, and then to test your knowledge of them. Specific directions for the various chapters are inserted at appropriate places.

The right-hand column of each page is a self-teaching section. As you read it, you will be asked to fill in the correct word or to interpret the meaning of a word or word part, on the basis of what you've learned so far in the unit. You'll find that you learn best if you actually write out the answer. Then look across to the left-hand column of the page for the correct answer. If your answer doesn't agree with the one given, review the material. Always be sure you understand the answer before you go on.

This self-teaching format allows you to find out immediately how well you can use and understand the new material in each unit. You can work as fast or as slowly as you wish. A good rule to follow is this: when the material is easy or when you are already familiar with it, work rapidly; when it becomes more difficult, slow down enough that you are really concentrating on what's new.

Each unit has been designed for approximately fifteen minutes. People differing as they do, it may take you more or less time. Do not worry about that. Just remember to complete a full unit at each time; do not break in the middle of a unit. It is probably unwise to work in this book for more than an hour. Relax or change to some other activity and give your mind a chance to fully absorb what you have learned.

Each chapter opens with a drawing illustrating some of the concepts or word parts covered in the chapter. As you read, you may enjoy turning back to the drawings to get their full meaning. For future reference, the Appendix lists the most important word parts and their meanings. The Index gives page references for each word part featured in a unit, so you can review the full discussion at any time.

At the end of the book is a final test. If you wish, you may take the test before you start reading the book and again afterward, to see how much you have learned. Otherwise, begin with Chapter 1.

Contents

CHAPTER ONE
Word Parts

This chapter introduces the word part approach that will be used throughout this book. The Information Panel on the next page is to be used as you read through this first chapter. First, read the Information Panel carefully. Then begin reading the right-hand column below, covering up the left-hand column with your hand or a piece of paper. When you come to an answer blank or question, write your answer in the space provided. Whenever helpful, look back at the Information Panel. Then check the book's answer in the left-hand column, on the same line. If you have answered correctly, continue reading. If not, reread the previous few lines. Often you can see a part that you misread or overlooked. Correct your answer and then go on.

	According to the panel, every English word contains
root	a word part or basic meaning called a _____.
	A word part placed in front of a root is called a
prefix	_____. In the word reshape, the root is
re	shape and the prefix is _____.
	The prefix re often has the meaning "again." Thus,
again	reread means "read _____," and reshape
again	means "shape _____."
arrange again	What does rearrange mean? _____
	If a woman wished to style her hair in a different way,
restyle	she would _____ it. (put together two word parts that mean "style again")
re	The word reclean divides into the prefix _____
clean	and the root _____ and means
clean again	"_____."
	The combination re is not a prefix unless it is placed before a root whose meaning it can change. In the

INFORMATION PANEL ON WORD PARTS

Every word in English has a root or basic meaning. Often, the root itself forms a complete word, such as <u>sure</u> or <u>shape</u>, but a root may also be a unit that is not used by itself, such as <u>dict</u> (say) in the word <u>predict</u>.

A prefix is a word part placed in front of a root to change the meaning. Examples are <u>unsure</u> (un + sure), <u>reshape</u> (re + shape), and <u>predict</u> (pre + dict). The prefixes added in the examples change the meaning: <u>unsure</u> means "not sure," <u>reshape</u> means "shape again," and <u>predict</u> means "say before" (that is, "say ahead of time").

More than one prefix can be placed in front of a prefix:

<u>renew</u> (re + new) = to make new again

<u>nonrenewable</u> (non + re + newable) = not able to be renewed

A suffix is a word part placed after a root. It tells us whether a word is being used as a noun, a verb, an adjective, or an adverb. Here are examples:

Nouns: <u>coolness</u> (cool + ness), <u>amusement</u> (amuse + ment), <u>diction</u> (dict + ion)
Verbs: <u>dictate</u> (dict + ate), <u>terrorize</u> (terror + ize), <u>walking</u> (walk + ing)
Adjectives: <u>joyous</u> (joy + ous), <u>useful</u> (use + ful), <u>restless</u> (rest + less)
Adverbs: <u>quickly</u> (quick + ly), <u>tamely</u> (tame + ly)

More than one suffix can be placed after a root. A word existing as one part of speech can be changed to another by adding an additional suffix.

Adjective: <u>helpful</u> (help + ful)
Adverb: <u>helpfully</u> (help + ful + ly)
Noun: <u>helpfulness</u> (help + ful + ness)

Many different words with different meanings can be formed merely by adding various prefixes and suffixes to a root. These words are called derivatives. Below are just a few of the derivatives of the root <u>ject</u>, which means "to throw."

project	projectile	interjection
projected	eject	conjecture
projecting	ejected	conjectural
projection	ejecting	reject
projectionist	ejection	
projector	interject	

Words may also be formed by putting two roots together.

<u>thermometer</u> = thermo (heat) + meter (measure) = that which measures heat
<u>democracy</u> = demo (people) + cracy (rule) = rule by the people

word red, re is not a prefix because there is no root for it to change: (re + d). Neither is it a prefix in the word rent (re + nt). Now test the word ready to see if it contains the prefix re: (re + ady). Do you

no · recognize ady as a word you already know? _____
Does it help explain the meaning of the larger word

no/no ready? _____ Is re, then, a prefix in ready? ___

The prefix pre often means "ahead of time." Apply this rule-of-thumb test for a prefix to these three words: press, preview, preach. In which word does

preview pre occur as a prefix? _____

view ahead of time The word preview means "_____."
Not all roots make complete words in themselves. In the information panel, for example, you are given several words derived from the root dict, meaning "say." Now look at the word recur, derived from the root cur, meaning "run." When re is added to

again cur, the expanded meaning becomes "run _____."
If an illness is likely to "run (its course) again," we

recur say that it may _____.

The prefix un means "not." When added to the root

certain, it makes a new word meaning

not certain "_____."

What would you add in front of the root seen to give

un the meaning "not seen"? _____

Under and untrue both begin with the combination un,

untrue but it is a prefix only in the word _____,

not true meaning "_____."

happy In the word unhappy the root is _____, the

un prefix is _____, and the meaning is

not happy "_____."

More than one prefix can be placed in front of a root. A medicine that can be refilled without another pre-scription is refillable (re + fillable)—literally, able to be filled again. If non means "not," form the word that means "not able to be filled again."

nonrefillable _____

non	The two prefixes added to <u>nonrefillable</u> are _____
re	and _____. <u>Nonrefillable</u> illustrates the principle that (write the correct choice):
more than one	only one/more than one _____ prefix can be added in front of a root.
	Now look at the panel. A part added after a root is
suffix	called a _____. It indicates whether a word is being used as a noun, a verb, an adjective, or an adverb.
	In the word <u>coolness</u> the root is <u>cool</u> and the suffix
ness	must therefore be _____.
amuse	In the word <u>amusement</u> the root is _____ and
ment	the suffix is _____.
	The suffix <u>ment</u> often has the meaning "act of." Thus, <u>argument</u> (argue + ment)* means "act of arguing" and would be used as a noun: Her <u>argument</u> is logical. In
judge	the word <u>judgment</u> the root is _____, the
ment	suffix is _____, and the meaning of the word
act of judging	is "_____."
	The suffix <u>ment</u> indicates that <u>judgment</u> is being used as what part of speech? (Check the panel if you're
a noun	not sure.) _____
	Another common suffix is <u>ness</u>. If you are very hap-
ness	py, you are in a "state of happi_____." If you dislike things that are ugly, you dislike their
ugliness	_____. (Using <u>ness</u>, give the noun form of <u>ugly</u>.)
	Still another common noun suffix is <u>ion</u>. Someone warns you to watch your <u>diction</u> because you are on television. The root is <u>dict</u> (say) and the suffix is <u>ion</u>. If <u>ion</u> means "act of," then <u>diction</u> is literally
the act of saying dict—say/ion—act of	"_____." (Note: Word

*Often as words are formed, letters are dropped or changed, as the <u>e</u> is dropped here. We will focus on the meaning of the new words. A useful guide to their spelling is SPELLING FOR ADULTS, another Self-Teaching Guide, by Charles Ryan.

meanings do change. This literal meaning is a bridge to the current dictionary definition—"the process of choosing words, especially the correct or acceptable words.")

To predict something that is going to happen is literally to "say ahead of time." If ion is added to this form of the word, you have changed it to prediction,

saying ahead of time

with the meaning "act of _____."

Sometimes a root itself indicates the part of speech. For example, we need no suffix to tell us that true is an adjective. Similarly, predict does not contain a suffix, yet it is used as a verb: I predict rain for tomorrow. The suffix ed is added to form the past tense: I predicted rain yesterday. Change the verb reject from the present tense to the past tense.

rejected

_____

A common verb suffix is ate, as in dictate. There is no literal meaning for ate; it simply indicates that the meaning of the word should be cast in the form of a verb: dict (say) + ate = to say. The verb cogitate would break down into the root cogit (think) + ate and

to think

would mean "_____."

Since dictate already ends in the letter e, only the letter d is needed to make the past tense form: dictate + d = dictated. Form the past tense of cogitate.

cogitated

_____

The verb terrorize means "to cause terror." If the

ize

root is terror, then the verb suffix is _____.

terrorized

The past tense of terrorize would be _____.

To indicate that an action continues to occur, the suffix ing is added: The weatherman is predicting rain for the weekend. Complete the verb form in the following sentence so that it will mean the action has

continued to occur: The monster has been _____

terrorizing

_____ the countryside for four weeks. (Use the proper form of terrorize.)

Adjective word forms are generally indicated by suffixes such as able, ful, and ous. A capable (cap + able) man is "able to do" things; material that is "able to be used" is usable. A plan that is "able to

workable

work" is _____.

The adjective suffix <u>ous</u> means "marked by." A <u>courageous</u> (courage + ous) soldier is "marked by courage." An <u>advantageous</u> (advantage + ous) remark is "marked by advantage." Form the word that means "marked by hazard" and could be used to describe road conditions after a storm.

hazardous

_____

The adjective suffix <u>ful</u> means "full of." <u>Helpful</u> (help + ful) means "full of help"; <u>harmful</u> means "full of harm." Form the word that means "full of

spiteful

spite." _____

Adverbial word forms are most commonly indicated by the ending <u>ly</u> after roots or after adjective suffixes: tame + ly, helpful + ly. What is the adverbial

purposefully

form of purposeful? _____

The suffix <u>ly</u> can mean the manner in which something is done (He spoke <u>softly</u>) or it can show degree (She was <u>extremely</u> happy). Fill in the adverbial form of <u>routine</u> in the following sentence: Jane did

routinely

the housework _____.

In the following sentence fill in the adverbial form of <u>unusual</u> that tells to what degree Harry was sad: Harry blamed himself for the mistake and felt

unusually

_____ sad.

Now apply what you have learned to a cluster of words derived from the root <u>ject</u>, meaning "throw." Consider the word <u>project</u>, as in "Henry tried to <u>project</u> a feeling of hope to the crowd." If the prefix <u>pro</u> means "forward," then the literal meaning of <u>project</u>

throw forward

is "to _____."

Consider the word <u>projection</u>, as in "His voice projection was not strong enough." If the suffix <u>ion</u> means "act of," then the literal meaning of <u>projection</u>

act of throwing
  forward

is "_____."

If the suffix <u>or</u> means "that which," what word stands for a machine used to "throw forward" images onto a

projector

screen? _____

If <u>ist</u> means "one who," what word is used to name

the person who is responsible for the <u>projection</u> of

projectionist

images onto a screen? _____

If <u>ile</u> is a noun suffix meaning "that which," supply
the word that fits the following sentence and means
"that which is thrown forward": A bullet is one type

projectile

of _____ manufactured by this
company.

A bartender tried to <u>eject</u> a misbehaving patron. If
<u>e</u> means "out," what did the bartender try to do?

throw out the patron

_____

Fill in the past tense form of <u>eject</u>: Last evening the

ejected

bartender _____ three rowdy persons.

Fill in the form of <u>eject</u> that shows action continuing

ejecting

to occur: The bartender has been _____
me right after my third drink.

The prefix <u>inter</u> means "between." If you throw a
witty remark into a conversation (between other peo-

interject

ple's remarks), you can be said to _____ it.

Charley Brown is fond of saying "Good grief!" This
expression conveys emotion rather than thought and
gives the impression of being thrown between statements that convey ideas. <u>Inter</u> means "between."
An expression such as "Good grief!" would therefore

interjection

be called an _____.

What happened to the money is a matter for <u>conjecture</u>.
In this sentence, <u>conjecture</u> means "that which is
thrown together." This literal meaning should lead
you to a current dictionary definition. Is <u>conjecture</u>
a "guess" or a "carefully reasoned explanation"?

a guess

_____

In the sentence "My remarks about the election are
only conjectural," the word <u>conjectural</u> describes
<u>remarks</u> (conjectural remarks). The suffix <u>al</u> must

adjective

therefore indicate an _____ word form.

In the sentence "He spoke conjecturally," the suffix
<u>ly</u> has been added to <u>conjectural</u> and tells the manner
in which he spoke. The word <u>conjecturally</u> must

adverbial

therefore be an _____ word form.

Two roots are sometimes combined to form a word, as in <u>thermometer</u> (thermo, "heat" + meter, "measure"). <u>Thermoelectricity</u> (thermo + electricity) would

heat

be "electricity produced directly by _____."
If <u>tele</u> means "far or distant," an instrument that measures great distances (in space) is called a

telemeter

_____.

Self-Test

1. Every word in English must contain a _____ or basic meaning.

2. A word part placed in front of a root to change its meaning is called a

   _____.

3. In the word <u>preheat</u> the prefix is _____ and the root is _____.

4. More than one prefix can be placed in front of a root. True or False?

   _____

5. How many prefixes are there in <u>nonrepayable</u>? _____

6. A word part placed after a root to indicate the part of speech is called a

   _____.

7. In the word <u>dictate</u> the suffix is _____.

8. In the word <u>predictable</u> the prefix is _____, the root is _____, and the suffix is _____.

9. In which word is <u>pre</u> used as a prefix? <u>predetermine</u>, <u>prey</u>, <u>precious</u>

   _____

10. More than one suffix can be placed after a root. True or False? _____

11. In the word <u>helpfully</u> the suffixes are _____ and _____.

12. By adding various prefixes and suffixes, many different words with different meanings can be formed from a single root. True or False? _____

13. <u>Eject</u> means "throw out"; <u>interject</u> means "throw between"; if <u>pro</u> means "forward," <u>project</u> means "_____."

14. Two roots can be combined to form a word. True or False? _____

15. The word <u>thermometer</u> contains how many roots? _____

Answers to Self-Test

1. root 2. prefix 3. pre/heat 4. True 5. two 6. suffix 7. ate 8. pre/dict/able 9. predetermine 10. True 11. ful/ly 12. True 13. throw forward 14. True 15. two

Now that you've completed this chapter, you might enjoy a new look at the drawing that opens it on page x.

CHAPTER TWO
Greek Roots

DIRECTIONS

Glance briefly at unit 1. Unit 1, like all the other units in Chapters 2 through 6, is divided into three sections: pronunciation, self-teaching section, and a self-test. For each unit, you should:

(1) Study carefully the word part that heads up each unit, paying special attention to the English meaning assigned to it.

(2) Pronounce the words derived from the word part. Say the derivatives out loud if at all possible. Research indicates that being able to pronounce a word is a vital ingredient in mastering it. A simplified method of showing pronunciation is used. Here are some examples based on everyday words you already know. The syllable printed in capital letters is accented.

acting (AK ting)	practical (PRAK tee kuhl)
insured (in SHURD)	idol (EYE duhl)
retarded (ree TARD ud)	vital (VEYE tuhl)
city (SIT ee)	mama (MAH muh)
easy (EE zee)	drama (DRAHM uh)
misery (MIZ er ee)	able (AY buhl)
ago (uh GO)	generation (gen er AY shun)
category (KAT uh gore ee)	indication (in duh KAY shun)
sofa (SO fuh)	

(3) With a piece of paper, cardboard, or your hand, cover the answers at the left side of the self-teaching section.

(4) Read through the self-teaching section and fill in your answer in each blank provided. The lists at the beginning of each unit contain all the information you will need in the self-teaching section.

(5) After you complete each question, check the answer given on the same line in the left-hand column. If you made a mistake, correct it and reread the item to find any clue you overlooked.

(6) When you have finished the self-teaching section, go on to the brief unit Self-Test that follows it. Fill in the word or meaning from that unit that best fits the sentence context. When you have finished all the items, check the

answers which follow. If you made a mistake, correct it and reread the sentence carefully to find the clue you overlooked. Occasionally you may need to look back at the unit to see how the word was originally defined or used.

Briefly, again, here are the directions:

Pronounce the words derived from the word part.
Cover the answer column.
Read and complete the self-teaching section.
Check your answers.
Correct any mistakes.
Take the Self-Test.

Now begin with unit 1 on the following page.

(1)   ANTHROP, ANTHROPO, man, mankind

Derivatives:

anthropocentric (an thruh puh CEN trik)
anthropophagus (an thruh PAHF uh gus)
anthropological (an thruh puh LODGE uh kuhl)
anthropologist (an thruh PAHL uh just)
anthropology (an thruh PAHL uh gee)
anthropoid (AN thruh poid)
misanthrope (MISS un thrope)
philanthropical (fill un THROP uh kuhl)
philanthropist (fuh LAN thruh puhst)
philanthropy (fuh LAN thruh pee)

Prefixes	Other roots	Suffixes
phil—love	logy—study of	ic, ical—related to
	mis—hate	ist—one who
	phagus—eater	oid—like, resembling
		y—act of

Margaret Mead always had a strong interest in learning about the races, customs, and beliefs of mankind.

anthropology
  anthropo—man
  logy—study of

In college she majored in _____.
(study of mankind)

She did research among the Trobrian Islanders of the South Pacific, published a book, and soon became a

anthropologist
  anthropo—man
  logy—study of
  ist—one who

famous _____. (one who studies mankind)

She tends to view current social problems from a(n)

anthropological

_____ viewpoint or perspective. (related to anthropology)

Chimpanzees and gorillas are classified as <u>anthropoid</u>

They resemble man; they are man-like.
  anthrop—man
  oid—resembling

apes. What does the word tell you about them? ____

_____

loves
  phil—love

A <u>philanthropist</u> is "one who _____ mankind." He usually shows this feeling by some form of practical help, such as service to others or a gift of money. The act of showing love in this manner is called

philanthropy

_____.

philanthropical

Charitable enterprises such as free clinics and soup kitchens and orphanages are called _____ endeavors. (related to philanthropy)

Scrooge in Dickens's A CHRISTMAS CAROL is a <u>mis-anthrope</u>. How does Scrooge feel toward his fellow

he hates mankind
mis—hate
anthrop—man

man? _____

A cannibal eats human flesh. So does a man-eater.

anthropophagus

What is a more academic term? _____

What adjective would you use to describe the outlook of a person who considers man to be the most signif-icant thing in the universe—that is, to be the center

anthropocentric

of it? a(n) _____ outlook

Self-Test

1. His generosity in donating money to worthy causes quickly earned him a reputation as a <u>philanthropist</u>. His gifts showed what kind of feeling to-ward people? _____

2. The TV special featured a young woman who had actually lived for a year among anthropoid apes. <u>Anthropoid</u> means _____.

3. Many developers and industrialists are indifferent about preserving the ecology. They concentrate their attention on man and his immediate needs. Their viewpoint is entirely _____. (man-centered)

4. At the moment I am so low on funds that giving you five dollars would have to be considered an act of _____. (act of showing love for mankind)

5. The academic term for "man-eater" is _____.

6. What is a <u>misanthrope</u>? A person who _____.

7. <u>Anthropology</u> is the _____.

8. Because she traveled with her father when he made his famous studies of North American Indian tribes, Miss Van Pelt considers herself a(n) _____. (one who studies mankind)

9. Most of Miss Van Pelt's _____ insights are her father's, not her own. (relating to the study of mankind)

10. As his great fortune dwindled and his health failed, Mr. Greaves was less

and less inclined to be _____. (related to acts of
showing love for mankind)

Answers to Self-Test

1. love 2. resembling man (man-like) 3. anthropocentric 4. philanthropy
5. anthropophagus 6. hates people (mankind) 7. study of mankind 8. anthropologist 9. anthropological 10. philanthropical

(2)   ARCH, first, ancient, chief

Derivatives:

archaic (ar KAY ik)	archetype (ARK uh type)
archangel (ARK ain juhl)	archfiend (ARCH FEEND)
archbishop (ARCH bish up)	architect (ARK uh tekt)
archeology (ar kee AHL uh gee)	monarchy (MON ar kee)
archeologist (ar kee AHL uh just)	oligarchy (AHL uh gar kee)

Prefixes	Other roots	Suffixes
mon—one	logy—study of	ist—one who
	olig—few	y—state of
	tect—builder	ic—related to

archfiend

Sherlock Holmes had one great enemy, Professor Moriarty, whom he considered to be a(n) _____

_____. (chief fiend)

archangel

In the Old Testament, Gabriel is a chief angel or

_____.

ancient; old-fashioned

According to some feminists, male courtesies such as opening doors for women are archaic. In this context archaic means _____.

architect

The chief builder in the construction of a building is the _____. (He is also the first builder.)

a chief one (king or ruler)

A monarchy is a government controlled by _____

_____.

archeology
 arch—ancient
 log—study of
 y—act of

The study of ancient civilizations, carried on particularly by excavating and describing ruins, is called

_____.

A person trained to excavate ruins and reconstruct the life of ancient civilizations is called a(n)

archeologist

_____.

A historian says that for ten years a certain European nation was in the hands of an <u>oligarchy</u> devoted to its own selfish purposes. Who exercises control in

a chief few; a small group of powerful people

an oligarchy? _____

An industrial exhibit tracing the history of the automobile called the Model T Ford the <u>archetype</u> of the mass-produced car in America. In view of this context, which of the following is a better definition? Underline your choice: a very important type/the original pattern from which copies were made.

the original pattern from which copies were made

archbishop

A chief bishop is a(n) _____.

Self-Test

1. Because designing a building is the first step in its construction, the person who does it is known as the _____. (chief builder)

2. The fort built by Sir Francis Drake when he first visited the California coast is believed to have been discovered by three amateur _____

   _____. (those who study ancient civilizations)

3. The pronouns <u>thee</u> and <u>thou</u> are no longer used and are considered to be

   _____. (ancient, old-fashioned)

4. Police believe the murders to be the work of a(n) _____.
   (chief fiend)

5. The twelve men seized control of the government, and it remained an oligarchy for twenty-one years. What does <u>oligarchy</u> mean? _____

   _____

6. As a two-fisted, hard-riding, independent-minded Western hero, John Wayne has probably achieved the status of a(n) _____.
   (chief type)

7. A bishop of the highest rank is a(n) _____.

8. Before the rebellion against heaven, Satan was the most important of the archangels. What does <u>archangel</u> mean? _____

9. What is <u>archeology</u>? _____

10. Only a few of the older statesmen were still in favor of retaining the monarchy. What does <u>monarchy</u> mean? _____

<u>Answers to Self-Test</u>

1. architect 2. archeologists 3. archaic 4. archfiend 5. rule by a chief few 6. archetype 7. archbishop 8. a chief, or top-ranking, angel 9. the study of ancient civilizations 10. one-man rule; government headed by a king

(3) CHRON, time

Derivatives:
  anachronism (uh NAK run izm)   chronology (kron AHL uh gee)
  anachronistic (uh nak run IST ik) chronological (kron uh LODGE uh kuhl)
  chronic (KRON ik)   chronologically (kron uh LODGE uh klee)
  chronicle (KRON uh kuhl)   chronometer (kruh NOM uh ter)
  chronicler (KRON uh kler)   synchronize (SIN kruh nize)

Prefixes	Other roots	Suffixes
ana—against	logy—discussion	(e)r—one who
syn—together	meter—that which measures	ic, ical—relating to
		ly—manner of
		ize—verb ending (do what the root says)
		ism—that which

An illness that lasts over a long period of time is a

chronic
  chron—time
  ic—relating to
_____ illness. (relating to time)

An extremely accurate clock used in scientific re-

chronometer
  chron—time
  meter—measure
search is called a _____.
(that which measures time)

If two dancers <u>synchronize</u> their movements, how do

together in time
  syn—together
  chron—time
they move? _____

In the cartoon strip Alley Oop, Alley is a primitive man from the Stone Age who is transported into the twentieth century and must cope with its problems.

anachronism
Most of the humor is based on this _____.
(that which is against the time sequence; a throwback in time)

The townspeople were wearing ancient costumes, there was a complete absence of cars and bicycles, and not a telephone wire or television aerial was to be seen. To an unsuspecting tourist who did not know it was a festival day, the town of Aldermaas would have been a truly anachronistic scene. What does

a throwback in time; against the normal time sequence

anachronistic mean? _____

A critic reads a biography and claims that the author's chronology of data is inaccurate. What does the critic claim about the data? That the data about

not in the right time order

someone's life is _____.

In writing a biography you would discuss events in the order in which they occurred; that is, you would

chronological

discuss them in _____ order. (relating to something based on a time sequence)

The events leading up to and causing World War I were listed chronologically. In what manner were

in a time sequence; in the order they occurred

the events listed? _____

A chronicler would be a person who records events

time order; order of occurrence

in what order? _____

A historical account that records events in their order of occurrence, usually without interpreting them,

chronicle

is called a _____. (that which is based on time)

Self-Test

1. Each time the liner passed into another time zone, Mr. Hawkins would

    set his ten-dollar wristwatch by the ship's _____.
    (that which measures time)

2. Six years after leaving the jungle he still suffered from a chronic skin

    rash. What does chronic mean here? _____

3. It was an _____ to be listening to rock and roll
    music as our raft took us past canyon walls that had existed a million years
    ago. (a throwback in time)

4. The details of Roger's adventure were set forth in _____
    order. (relating to time sequence)

5. It would be anachronistic to look out the window and see herds of buffalo grazing on the front lawn! Anachronistic means _____

    _____

6. Before hitting the beach, the sergeant told the men to synchronize their watches with his. What did he tell them to do? _____

    _____

7. The application asked us to list our former jobs chronologically. Our former jobs should be listed in what manner? _____

8. The Hellstrom Chronicle is a science-fiction account of how insects are prepared to take over the world. What is a chronicle? _____

    _____

9. Professor Durio's chief scholarly contribution was to have worked out a reasonably accurate _____ of the known facts about Shakespeare. (discussion based on time sequence)

10. Sir Rounfall's account of the War of the Roses is full of opinion and personal judgment, as he knew; he never claimed to be merely a chronicler. What is a chronicler? _____

Answers to Self-Test

1. chronometer 2. lasting over a long period of time 3. anachronism
4. chronological 5. relating to a throwback in time 6. set their watches at the same time 7. in order as the jobs were held 8. an account of events in the order in which they occurred, usually without interpretation 9. chronology 10. a person who records events in the order in which they occurred without interpreting them

(4)   DEM, DEMO, people

Derivatives:

demagogue (DEM uh gog)   demography (duh MOG ruh fee)
demagoguery (DEM uh gog ree)   endemic (en DEM ik)
democracy (duh MOK ruh see)   epidemic (ep uh DEM ik)
demographer (duh MOG ruh fer)   pandemic (pan DEM ik)

Prefixes	Other roots	Suffixes
en—within	crac—rule	(e)ry—act of
epi—above, upon	gogue—leader	ic—relating to, being
pan—all	graph—record	y—act of

people
  demo—people
  crac—rule
  y—act of

Democracy means rule by the _____.

people
  epi—upon
  dem—people
  ic—relating to

Even though the word epidemic means "upon the
_____," it is used to describe an outbreak
of disease that affects slightly less than ten percent
of the population.

all
  pan—all
  dem—people

Even though pandemic means "_____ the
people," it is used to describe an outbreak of disease
that affects slightly more than ten percent of the pop-

pandemic

ulation. Thus, a(n) _____ disease

epidemic

is more widespread than a(n) _____
disease.

You come across a newspaper article with the statement that the common cold is endemic in America.
You know that it means "being within a people."
Keeping the context and the literal meaning in mind,
underline the current meaning you think most likely

regularly occurring
in a particular
people or locality

grew out of it: regularly occurring in a particular
people or locality/causing illness to a portion of the
people only. Character traits may also seem to be
inborn. Some tourists believe that laziness is

endemic

_____ in tropical countries.
(being within a people)

people leader
(leader of people)

Demagogue means "_____."
The word originated at a time when the people were
considered to be an ignorant, undiscerning, easily
led mob. A demagogue leads people by appealing to
their hatreds and prejudices rather than to their ide-
alism and reason. He also stirs up people to gain
his own ends, not theirs. If you accused a political
candidate or office-holder of demagoguery, would he

very insulted!

be insulted or flattered? _____

The "science of recording people" is known as

demography
  demo—people
  graph—record

_____.

The U. S. Government employs a great many demographers who conduct a census of the population every
ten years. Keeping in mind this context and also the
literal meaning "those who record people," which do
you think is the current meaning of demographer:

those who collect and study vital statistics...

those who write official letters for people unable to do so for themselves/those who collect and study vital statistics about a people.

Self-Test

1. According to the popular notion, thriftiness and frugality are supposed to be endemic to Scotsmen. <u>Endemic</u> means _____.

2. A counselor suggested that Jason might be happy majoring in demography, which is the science of _____.

3. His campaign speech was so full of hate and prejudice and so lacking in logic that I feel justified in calling him a demagogue. A <u>demagogue</u> is

_____.

4. Today many advertisers rely heavily on the findings of _____.
(those who collect and evaluate statistical data about people)

5. When slightly less than ten percent of the population is suffering from a disease, the public health authorities say it is _____.
(upon the people)

6. The newspaper columnist said that liberal people should regard Senator Fogbound's election defeat as the rejection of _____
in Midwestern politics. (act of leading the people by the wrong methods and principles)

7. In some parts of the country venereal disease has become so extremely widespread among teenagers that it is no longer just epidemic but instead

_____. (being in "all" the people)

8. A one-party system hardly seems suitable if a country really wishes to call itself a _____. (rule by the people)

Answers to Self-Test

1. being within the people; inborn 2. collecting and evaluating data about populations 3. a politician who leads people by their prejudices for his own ends 4. demographers 5. epidemic 6. demagoguery 7. pandemic 8. democracy

⑤ DOX, belief, teaching, opinion

Derivatives:

doxology (dox AHL uh gee)
heterodox (HET er uh dox)
orthodox (ORTH uh dox)
orthodoxy (ORTH uh dox ee)

paradox (PEAR uh dox)
paradoxical (pear uh DOX uh kuhl)
paradoxically (pear uh DOX ik lee)

Prefixes
hetero—different
ortho—correct
para—alongside

Other roots
logy—words of

Suffixes
ical—characterized by
ly—manner of
y—state of

words of belief
  dox—belief
  logy—words of

What is the literal meaning of doxology? _____

_____

A regular feature of some religious services is to

doxology

sing or recite the _____.
(words of belief)

What is the literal meaning of orthodox? Of or having

the correct belief
  ortho—correct
  dox—belief

_____. Suppose you share
the majority belief about the importance of the family
unit; most people would consider your opinion to be

orthodox

_____ or conventional.

A candidate for office who belongs to a major political
party and supports conventional measures is staying

orthodoxy

within the guidelines of political _____.
(condition of following correct beliefs)

What is the literal meaning of heterodox? Being of a

different belief
  hetero—different
  dox—belief

_____. If your opinions
differ markedly from the conventional ones, they

heterodox

would be labeled _____.
(of a different belief)

Suppose there are two theories to explain what light
is. Both theories seem to be equally supportable.

paradox
  para—alongside
  dox—belief

This situation constitutes a _____.
(beliefs alongside each other) It means that the two
opinions contradict each other. Thomas Jefferson
was the product of a privileged class, yet he strongly
believed in democracy as the best form of government.

paradoxical

Historians often call attention to this _____
fact. (relating to beliefs that exist alongside each
other) To phrase it differently, Thomas Jefferson
would have been expected to support a government
ruled by a few wealthy, influential men, but

paradoxically

_____ he did not.
(manner of two beliefs existing alongside each other
and contradicting each other)

Self-Test

1. Miss Thurmond had no taste for controversy, and she ran the school for young ladies in an <u>orthodox</u> fashion. That is, she ran her school in what way? _____

2. Elizabeth slipped into a back pew just as the congregation rose to its feet to sing the doxology. <u>Doxology</u> means _____.

3. Man appears to have a _____ nature: one part of him yearns for union with the group, while another part strongly demands freedom and individuality. (characterized by conflicting beliefs)

4. The true liberal behaves _____; he may despise your opinions but he will defend with his life your right to express them. (manner of behaving as though one held opposed beliefs)

5. The American Medical Association did not receive Dr. Kramer well because of his heterodox ideas about the practice of healing. <u>Heterodox</u> means his ideas were _____.

6. In his writing Hawthorne was continually probing the moral paradox that good comes out of evil and evil comes out of good. A <u>paradox</u> is _____

_____.

7. At 18 he was drawn to revolution; at 25 he admitted to some radicalism; at 30 he had completely slipped back into the comfortable lap of political

_____. (correct beliefs)

Answers to Self-Test

1. conventionally; based on "correct belief" 2. words of belief 3. paradoxical 4. paradoxically 5. characterized by different beliefs; unconventional 6. an apparent contradiction of beliefs 7. orthodoxy

(6) DYNA, power

Derivatives:
dynamic (deye NAM ik)
dynamics (deye NAM iks)
dynamite (DEYE nuh mite)
dynamo (DEYE nuh mo)

dynasty (DEYE nuss tee)
thermodynamics (THUR mo deye NAM iks)

Other roots
thermo—heat

Suffixes
ic—being
ics—operation of

Sir Malcolm has been described in the press as a dynamic lecturer.   What does <u>dynamic</u> mean?

being powerful or
effective

_____

The greatest perfection of Chinese art occurred during the nearly three hundred years of the Ming Dynasty. If Ming refers to a ruling family, what does

the time during
which the Mings
held power or
ruled

Ming <u>Dynasty</u> mean here? _____

_____

The school psychologist wrote her thesis on the dynamics of interpersonal relationships. Literally,

power

<u>dynamics</u> would be "the operation of _____."
This literal meaning would lead to the current definition: "the physical or moral forces at work in any field."

The bridge was blown up with dynamite. What part of the word <u>dynamite</u> tells you that it is an explosive

dyna

of great power or force? _____

At Hoover Dam each dynamo generates an incredible amount of electrical energy each day. If <u>dyna</u> can also mean "energy," then a <u>dynamo</u> is "that which

power (energy)

generates _____." A fuller definition would be "a machine that generates electricity by changing mechanical energy into electrical energy."
A person who is extremely energetic ("a real live-

dynamo

wire") may also be called a _____.

In a branch of physics called <u>thermodynamics</u>, you would study the relation between what forces?

heat and power
(electrical energy)

_____

Self-Test

1. After overcoming her early shyness, Thelma later became a talented and

dynamic actress. <u>Dynamic</u> here means _____.

2. Because two of President Kennedy's brothers held high offices, the Kennedy

Administration was jokingly referred to as the Kennedy _____.
(time during which a family rules)

3. In advertising his daring athletic feats, the circus billed him as "The Hu-

man _____." (that which generates power)

4. Roger said he had seen at first hand the _____ at work in the selection of a presidential candidate. (physical or moral forces at work in a field)

5. An old building of that type would have to be destroyed with _____. (explosive of great power or force)

6. Her brother, whose interests lay in physics, specialized in thermodynamics. What is <u>thermodynamics</u>? _____

Answers to Self-Test

1. powerful or effective 2. Dynasty 3. Dynamo 4. dynamics 5. dynamite 6. a branch of physics dealing with the relation between heat and electrical energy (power)

(7) GAM, marriage

Derivatives:
bigamist (BIG uh mist)
bigamy (BIG uh mee)
endogamy (en DOG uh mee)
exogamy (egg ZOG uh mee)
misogamist (mih SOG uh mist)

monogamist (muh NOG uh mist)
monogamous (muh NOG uh muss)
monogamy (muh NOG uh mee)
polygamy (puh LIG uh mee)

<u>Prefixes</u>
bi—two
en—within
exo—outside
mono—one
poly—many

<u>Other roots</u>
miso—hate

<u>Suffixes</u>
ist—one who
ous—based on
y—act

only one
mono—one
gam—marriage
ist—one who

monogamous

monogamy

A <u>monogamist</u> is a man or woman who enters into how many marriages at the same time? _____

A person who is reasonably conventional will seek to establish a _____ relationship with a mate. (based on one marriage at a time)

A monogamist believes in or practices _____

_____. (act of having one marriage)

In our culture a person caught being married to two

or more people at the same time is guilty of

bigamy
  bi—two
  gam—marriage
  y—act

_____. (act of having two marriages)

In fact, newspaper reporters will label such a person

bigamist

a _____. (one who has more than two marriages at the same time)

Some cultures allow a person to have more than one marriage at a time. When legal, such a practice is

polygamy

called _____. (act of many marriages)

Too many marriages within the same group can lead to physical defects. If <u>endo</u> means "within," another

endogamy

name for inbreeding is _____.

To maintain the vigor of the race, some groups require that young men take brides outside their own

exogamy

group, a practice called _____.

a person who
hates marriage

What is a misogamist? _____

_____

Self-Test

1. In the eyes of the court Julius was married to two women at once and was therefore a _____.

2. The marriage code of the Western nations is based on <u>monogamy</u>. That is, the code is based on _____.

3. Until very recently, at least, most American women have sought to establish _____ relationships. (based on one marriage)

4. In some parts of Africa wealthy men are not only allowed but are encouraged to practice polygamy. <u>Polygamy</u> is _____

_____.

5. Thinking to discourage her pursuit of him, Mr. Jones said, "Please, Miss Tuttle! I am a _____!" (one who practices one marriage at a time)

6. The old bachelor readily admitted that he was a misogamist. What did he

admit to? _____

7. His Mexican divorce was ruled invalid, and the court held that he was
    technically guilty of <u>bigamy</u> when he married his second wife, Susan.

    That is, he was guilty of _____.

8. Marriage inside one's own family or group is called _____.

9. According to custom, a young man had to kidnap his bride from a neigh-
    boring tribe—a device that ensured exogamy. <u>Exogamy</u> is _____

    _____.

Answers to Self-Test

1. bigamist 2. having only one marriage at a time 3. monogamous 4. act of
having many marriages at the same time 5. monogamist 6. hating marriage
7. having two wives at the same time 8. endogamy 9. marriage outside one's
own group

(8)   GEN, birth, race, kind

Derivatives:

congenital (kuhn JEN uh tuhl)   genocide (JEN uh side)
degenerate (dee JEN er ate)   genus (GEE nuss)
gene (JEEN)   photogenic (fote uh JEN ik)
genealogist (jeen ee AHL uh just) progenitor (pro JEN uh ter)
genealogy (jeen ee AHL uh gee)   progeny (PRAH jen ee)
generate (JEN er ate)   psychogenic (seye ko JEN ik)
genitals (JEN uh tulls)

Prefixes	Other roots	Suffixes
con—with	cid—kill	al—that which
de—reverse of	logy—study of	al—being
pro—forward	photo—light	ate—verb ending
	psych—mind	ist—one who
		or—one who
		us—that which
		y—that which

birth, race, or
kind

The germ cells that carry hereditary characteristics
from parent to offspring are called genes. <u>Genes</u>,
then, determine the characteristics of _____

_____.

A defect that is present "with birth" is said to be

_____.

congenital
  con—with
  gen—birth
  al—being

they gave you birth,
sent you forward into
the world or future

What do you think it means to say that your parents, grandparents, and great-grandparents are your

progenitors? _____

_____

it gives birth to
excitement

If a new piece of music generates excitement, what

does it do? _____

worse

If a plant or animal strain degenerates, does it become better or worse? _____

photogenic

Which of the derivatives might describe a person who

looks good in photographs? _____

race or kind

The genitals are the sexual organs that reproduce

the _____.

race
   gen—race
   cide—kill

Genocide is the intentional destruction of a _____,
but it can be extended to include social or political
groups.

genus

Botanists not only describe each plant as being a particular species but also classify it as a member of a larger family (kind) of plants known as a genus. For example, the Easter lily is known botanically as lilium

longiflorum, and it belongs to the _____
liliaceae.   (family of plants)

a person who traces
family origins

Hoping to discover famous forebears, some people
consult a genealogist, who will work out the family

tree.   What is a genealogist? _____

_____

genealogy

What is the study of family pedigrees called? _____

_____

birth

The literal meaning of progeny is something like this:

"that which has been given _____."
More simply, progeny are the offspring of plants or
animals.

psychogenic

All illness that appears to have been produced or created by a mental condition is said to be _____.
(having its origin in the mind)

Self-Test

1. My cousin, an amateur genealogist, says that some of our forebears greeted the Pilgrims. What does a genealogist do? _____

_____

2. The so-called meadow cowslip is <u>primula vulgaris</u>, which belongs to the _____ <u>primulaceae</u>. (family or kind)

3. Because they killed everyone in the town of Lidice, the Nazis were accused of genocide. <u>Genocide</u> means _____.

4. The Smiths' oldest son is afflicted with a _____ speech defect. (present with birth)

5. Your children will be your _____. (offspring; those given birth)

6. Your parents and grandparents are your _____. (those who gave you birth, sent you forth)

7. Some kinds of migraine headache are thought to be psychogenic in nature. <u>Psychogenic</u> means _____.

8. If the inbreeding is not stopped. this strain of cattle will _____. (become worse; lose some original quality)

9. Lawrence was so tired he said he must have _____ for laziness. (germ cells that carry hereditary characteristics)

10. Aunt Matilda always hides when it comes time for picture-taking. She says she is not photogenic. <u>Photogenic</u> describes someone who

_____.

11. Even very small children are fascinated with their _____ and ask questions about them. (reproductive organs)

12. The soaring price of gold generated new interest in prospecting in the old gold country. This means that interest in prospecting (underline the correct choice): increased/decreased/remained the same.

13. Simply by checking the names and dates on the family portraits that lined the hallways, Lady Margaret could easily trace her _____. (family origins)

Answers to Self-Test

1. traces family origins 2. genus 3. murder of a race or group 4. congenital
5. progeny 6. progenitors 7. originating in the mind 8. degenerate 9. genes
10. looks good in photographs 11. genitals 12. increased 13. genealogy

(9) HYDR, water

Derivatives:

hydrant (HEYE drunt)   hydrophyte (HEYE dro fite)
hydraulic (heye DRAW lik)   hydroponically (heye dro PON ik lee)
hydrophobia (heye dro FOE bee uh) hydroponics (heye dro PON iks)
hydroplane (HEYE dro plane)   hydrotherapy (heye dro THER uh pee)

Other roots   Suffixes
phobia—fear   ant—that which
phyte—plant   ic—related to
ponics—labor   ly—manner
therapy—cure,
    treatment

water   A fire _hydrant_ is a large outlet for _____ .

                             A plane that can land or take off on water is a

hydroplane   _____ .

water   A _hydraulic_ press is operated by _____
                             pressure.

a water plant   What is a _hydrophyte_? _____
  hydr—water
  phyte—plant

the use of water   What is _hydrotherapy_? _____
as a cure
                             The technical term for rabies is _hydrophobia_. The

water fear   literal meaning of _hydrophobia_ is "_____."
  hydr—water   A victim of this disease exhibits a morbid fear of
  phobia—fear   water because of the inability to swallow water or
                             liquids.

                             Rapid advances are being made in the relatively new
                             science of growing plants in water instead of soil. It

hydroponics   is called _____ . (water labor)
                             Hydroponics is usually conducted in a greenhouse.

                             Many vegetables and flowers are now being produced

hydroponically   _____ . (in a manner
                             based on water labor)

Self-Test

1. Most American automobiles now employ hydraulic rather than mechanical

    brakes. _Hydraulic_ brakes use what kind of pressure? _____

2. The hyacinths that choke irrigation ditches and rice paddies are examples of undesirable hydrophytes. What is a <u>hydrophyte</u>? _____

3. For John's lower back pain the doctor recommended swimming as an inexpensive form of _____. (use of water as a cure or treatment)

4. In short-season climates tomatoes have been as profitable when grown hydroponically as when grown on land. Plants grown <u>hydroponically</u> are grown in _____.

5. Small _____ bring mail, food, and supplies to these lonely Alaskan settlements. ("water planes")

6. The traffic ticket irritated her because she thought she had parked far enough away from the fire _____. (large water outlet)

7. _____, better known as rabies, is a viral disease transmitted to warm-blooded animals through bites. (fear of water)

8. Mr. Morton is building a large greenhouse in order to experiment with _____. (growing plants in water)

Answers to Self-Test

1. water pressure 2. a water plant 3. hydrotherapy 4. water 5. hydroplanes 6. hydrant 7. hydrophobia 8. hydroponics

(10) LOG, LOGY, speech, study of, collection of

Derivatives:

astrology (ass TRAHL uh gee)
cryptology (krip TAHL uh gee)
ichthyology (ik thee AHL uh gee)
ideological (id ee uh LODGE uh kuhl)
ideology (id ee AHL uh gee
logic (LODGE ik)

logomania (log oh MAIN ee uh)
monologue (MON uh log)
ornithology (orn uh THAHL uh gee)
technology (tek NAHL uh gee)
travelogue (TRAV uh log)
zoology (zoe AHL uh gee)

Prefixes	Other roots	Suffixes
mono—one	astro—star	ic—science of
dia—across	crypt—secret	ical—relating to
	ichthy—fish	
	ideo—idea	
	mania—madness	
	orn—bird	
	tech—skill	
	zoo—animal	

When two actors speak to each other across a stage, we say they are carrying on a dialogue ("speech across"). When one actor speaks alone on the stage, we call it a _____.

monologue
  mono—one
  log—speech

Which derivative means a lecture, often with illustrations, about visiting part of the world?

travelogue

_____

Sherlock Holmes used <u>logic</u> to solve crimes. Here the literal meaning of <u>logic</u>—the science of words— is not of much help unless you realize that <u>words</u> are used in reasoning. In an effort to prove something

logic

by reasoning, you would use _____.

Which derivative would mean abnormal talkativeness

logomania
  log—speech
  mania—madness

(a madness for speech)? _____

<u>Logy</u> also means "study of." For example. <u>biology</u> is the "study of life" and <u>psychology</u> is the "study of the mind." What is the meaning of the derivatives below?

study of animals   zoology _____

study of birds   ornithology _____

study of fishes   ichthyology _____
(Both ornithology and ichthyology are branches of zoology.)

study of stars   astrology _____

Astrology actually means a study of the stars for the purpose of reading character and forecasting events. Astronomy (which literally means "systematized knowledge of the stars") is considered to be a scientific study of the stars. Most scientists regard astrology as being a pseudo-science, or "false science." A fortune teller would give you a horoscope, or prediction of your future, on the basis of: astrology/

astrology

astronomy.

What derivative means "the study of secret mes-

cryptology

sages?" _____

<u>Logy</u> can also mean "collection of." What do we mean when we talk of a person's <u>ideology</u>? Write your answer in the blank on the following page.

collection of ideas
that makes up a
person's point of
view

_____

_____

ideological

If two people have quite different points of view, we say they have _____ differences. (relating to a collection of ideas)

technology

Which derivative means a collection of skills required to carry on industry? _____

Self-Test

1. The most successful intelligence code was developed by a man who knew practically nothing about <u>cryptology</u>, which is _____

   _____.

2. The _____ differences separating the East and the West are illustrated by their definitions of the word <u>democracy</u>. (relating to points of view)

3. Tim did not admit he was part of the family drama; as far as he was concerned, his father was delivering a monologue on personal responsibility. A <u>monologue</u> is _____.

4. His gift for sketching and his hobby of bird-watching naturally led him into the field of _____. (study of birds)

5. Her belief in astrology was so strong she would not get out of bed if her forecast was not right. What is <u>astrology</u>? _____

   _____.

6. His degree in ichthyology almost guaranteed him a promotion in the Department of Fish and Game. <u>Ichthyology</u> is _____.

7. The famous author denied that he had tried to further any political _____

   _____ whatsoever in his latest novel. (collection of ideas)

8. Perry Mason is noted for the kind of _____ he used in proving the innocence of his clients. (reasoning with words)

9. If a person has <u>logomania</u>, he _____.

10. A trade school might also be called a school of _____. (a collection of skills needed in industry)

11. From producing home movies he graduated to short-length travelogues.

A _travelogue_ is _____.

12. Nevin had studied enough _____ to be able to classify most of the creatures living in or near the pond. (study of animals)

Answers to Self-Test

1. the study of secret messages 2. ideological 3. a speech by one actor alone on the stage 4. ornithology 5. study of the stars for prediction and character reading 6. study of fish 7. ideology 8. logic 9. is abnormally talkative 10. technology 11. an illustrated lecture about travel 12. zoology

(11) MEGA, MEGALO, great   MICRO, small

Derivatives:

megaphone (MEG uh phone)
megalomania (meg uh lo MAIN ee uh)
megalomaniac (meg uh lo MAIN ee ak)
megalopolis (meg uh LOP uh liss)
megaton (MEG uh tuhn)
megavitamin (MEG uh VITE uh muhn)

microbe (MEYE krobe)
microcosm (MEYE kro kozm)
microfilm (MEYE kro film)
micrometer (meye KROM uh ter)
microorganism (meye kro OR gun izm)

Other roots
be—life
cosm—universe
mania—madness
meter—measure
phone—sound
polis—city

Suffixes
iac—one who

To help their voices carry farther, cheerleaders sometimes use _megaphones_. What do you think these instruments do? _____

increase the loudness of the voice

To have an abnormal desire to do great things is to suffer from _____.
(madness about doing great things)

megalomania

A person who suffers such an abnormality is a

megalomaniac

_____.

An atomic bomb with an explosive force equal to a million tons of dynamite would have a value of one

megaton

_____. ("great ton")

megalopolis

A great concentration of population, usually identified by its largest city, is called a _____.

microfilm

The use of _____ allows the printed page to be photographed in reduced size, thus decreasing the space needed for storing books, documents, reports, and the like.

microorganisms

Tiny germs or bacteria that cannot be seen except through a microscope are called _____.

microbes

They can also be called _____. (small life)

measures very
small things

An instrument that is often used with a microscope is a micrometer. What do you think a scientist does with a <u>micrometer</u>? _____

megavitamin

A great dose of vitamins—one many times the minimum daily requirement—is called a _____.

"small universe"

<u>Microcosm</u> means "_____."

a representation
in miniature

A speaker says, "A space ship is a microcosm of the civilization that launched it." Underline the definition of <u>microcosm</u> that best fits this context: a representation in miniature/just one small part

Self-Test

1. Most people who have studied him believe that Hitler suffered from

   _____. (an abnormal desire to do great things)

2. The Russians secretly exploded a 100-_____ bomb. ("great ton")

3. A virus is a disease-producing agent smaller than any known _____

   _____. (two words can fit here)

4. Most visitors think of the Greater Los Angeles Area as being a megalopolis. A <u>megalopolis</u> is _____.

5. Rudy Vallee, a popular singer during the twenties, sang through a <u>megaphone</u>, which is _____.

6. Harry is hardly a _____ just because he thinks he is the best ball player in the county!

7. A single drop of water from a pond, examined under the microscope, appears to be a microcosm of the biological laws affecting all life. What is a <u>microcosm</u>? _____

8. An instrument used to measure very small things being examined under

a microscope is a _____ .

9. In his book on health Dr. Linus Pauling uses himself as an example of the benefits to be derived from taking megavitamins. <u>Megavitamins</u> refers to

_____ .

10. The space needed for files is greatly reduced when record-keeping is

switched over to _____ . ("reduced film")

Answers to Self-Test

1. megalomania 2. megaton 3. microorganisms or microbes 4. a large concentration of population 5. a hornlike instrument for increasing sound 6. megalomaniac 7. a small universe; a representation in miniature 8. micrometer 9. large doses of vitamins, beyond the daily requirement 10. microfilm

(12) MORPH, form

Derivatives:

amorphous (uh MOR fuss)
anthropomorphic (an thruh puh MOR fik)
anthropomorphism (an thruh puh MORF izm)

metamorphosis (met uh MORF uh sis)
morphology (mor FAHL uh gee)
polymorphic (pahl uh MOR fik)
polymorphous (pahl uh MOR fuss)

Prefixes	Other roots	Suffixes
a—without	anthropo—man	ism—act of
meta—change	poly—many	ic—relating to
	logy—study of	osis—process
		ous—relating to, being

Caterpillars undergo a metamorphosis to become butterflies. The word parts tell us that <u>metamorpho-sis</u> means _____ .

process of change
in form
  meta—change
  morph—form
  osis—process

without form
  a—without
  morph—form
  ous—being

If your plans or ideas about something are <u>amorphous</u>, that means they are _____ .

form

Some people worship <u>anthropomorphic</u> deities. These are gods conceived in the _____ of man.

anthropomorphism

Because the Greeks and Romans worshipped man-like gods, a striking feature of their religion is _____. (act of worshipping man-like gods)

the form and structure

If a geologist, a linguist, or a biologist is studying <u>morphology</u>, each is studying what part of his subject? _____

different forms

polymorphous

If an organism or a substance is <u>polymorphic</u>, that means it has, occurs in, or assumes _____ _____. Another adjective with the same meaning is _____.

Self-Test

1. John's vacation plans are <u>amorphous</u>. What does that tell us about John's vacation plans? _____

2. After being carefully guided in her _____ by Professor Higgins, Eliza Doolittle, the Cockney flower girl, emerged as a poised, cultivated lady. (process of changing form)

3. An organism that occurs in or assumes many forms can be described with two adjectives: _____ or _____.

4. Their crude carvings and man-like idols indicated that these people worshipped anthropomorphic gods. <u>Anthropomorphic</u> means _____ _____.

5. The crude carvings and man-like idols were evidence of _____ _____. (noun form of <u>anthropomorphic</u>)

6. A branch of biology called <u>morphology</u> deals with the _____ _____ of plants and animals.

Answers to Self-Test

1. they are formless 2. metamorphosis 3. polymorphic or polymorphous
4. in the form of man 5. anthropomorphism 6. form and structure

(13)   NEO, new

Derivatives:
    neoclassical (knee uh KLASS uh   neolithic (knee uh LITH ik)
       kuhl)   neologism (knee uh LOW gizm)
    neocolonialism (knee uh kuh LONE   neophyte (KNEE uh fite)
      ee uhl izm)

Other roots	Suffixes
lith—stone	ic, ical—relating to
logism—word	
phyte—plant	

"new plant"   A <u>neophyte</u> is a "_____," but
neo—new   the word is used to identify a person newly initiated
phyte—plant   into something.

                The <u>neolithic</u> period, a time when primitive man advanced to using polished stone tools, literally means

new stone   the _____ age.
neo—new
lith—stone   Less than twenty years ago when it first came into
                existence as a word, <u>beatnik</u> was a neologism. What

a new word   does <u>neologism</u> mean? _____
neo—new
log—word   During the late seventeenth and early eighteenth century, many English artists and authors turned to the
                classical works of ancient Greece and Rome for their

neoclassical   inspiration. This period is known as the _____
                age. (new classical)

                If a large nation follows a policy of trying to dominate former colonies politically or economically, this

neocolonialism   practice is called _____.
                (new colonialism)

Self-Test

1.   The stone knife dated back to the neolithic period. <u>Neolithic</u> means

   _____.

2.   Maria eventually became a fine seamstress and an efficient housekeeper,

   but she always acted like a _____ in the kitchen.
   ("new plant")

3.   "Uptight" and similar neologisms usually have a life span of about twenty years. What is a <u>neologism</u>? _____

4.   Leaders of the revolution in the colony charged Portugal with following a policy of _____.

5.   Perhaps the most representative poetry of the _____ age was written by Alexander Pope. (relating to the new age of classical art)

<u>Answers to Self-Test</u>

1. new stone 2. neophyte 3. a new word 4. neocolonialism 5. neoclassical

(14)   NOM, rule, law, systematized knowledge

Derivatives:

agronomist (uh GRAHN uh mist)   astronomy (uh STRON uh mee)
agronomy (uh GRAHN uh mee)   autonomous (aw TAHN uh muss)
astronomer (uh STRON uh mer)   autonomy (aw TAHN uh mee)
astronomic (ass truh NOM ik)   metronome (MET ro nome)
astronomically (ass truh NOM
   ik lee)

<u>Other roots</u>	<u>Suffixes</u>
agr—field	ic—relating to
auto—self	ically—in a manner relating to
astr—star	ist—one who
metro—measure	er—one who
	ous—being
	y—(indicates word is a noun)

A clocklike device with a pendulum that can be adjusted to tick (keep time) at different speeds is a

metronome   _____. (that which "rules the measure")

Many former colonial possessions in Africa have achieved a state of <u>autonomy</u>—that is, they have a-

self-rule   chieved _____.
   auto—self
   nom—rule

A local school system that wishes to be completely free of interference from county, state, or federal

autonomous   officials wishes to be _____.
                           (relating to self-rule)

agronomy   The management of crop production is called _____
                           _____. ("rule of the field")

agronomist

Many large farm corporations now employ the services of an _____. (one who manages crop production)

astronomy
  astro—star
  nom—systematized
  knowledge

What field would you study to gain a systematized knowledge of the stars? _____

You may recall from an earlier unit that a person who "studies the stars" in order to make predictions about human events is an astrologer; but a scientific

astronomer

stargazer is an _____.

Since a study of the stars involves such fantastically high numbers in mathematics, we can speak of the

astronomic

high cost of something as being _____. (relating to knowledge of the stars)

prices are
fantastically
high

If we say that prices have risen astronomically, what do we mean? _____

Self-Test

1. Many mine operators wish they could return to the autonomy they enjoyed before the government was given regulatory powers over them. That is, they wish to return to _____.

2. The money involved in such a major undertaking is simply _____ _____. (involving fantastically high numbers or figures)

3. Countries that are undeveloped in agriculture are invited to send selected students to the university to study agronomy. What will they study?

   _____

4. The cost of maintaining the armed forces is rising _____ _____. (in a manner involving fantastically high figures)

5. Galileo was a famous Italian physicist and _____. (one who has systematized knowledge of the stars)

6. Although considered part of the larger educational system, each of the four colleges is fully _____. (self-governing)

7. Larry always practiced the piano with a metronome sitting nearby. What

does the <u>metronome</u> do? _____

8. The soil on our farm was tested by an _____. (one
    who manages crop production)

9. The study of the stars used to predict human events is called astrology;

    the scientific study of the stars is called _____.

Answers to Self-Test

1. self-rule 2. astronomic 3. crop management 4. astronomically 5. astronomer 6. autonomous 7. it keeps time 8. agronomist 9. astronomy

(15)   ONYM, name

Derivatives:

acronym (AK ro nim)	heteronym (HET er uh nim)
antonym (ANN tuh nim)	homonym (HAHM uh nim)
anonymity (ann uh NIM uh tee)	patronym (PAT ruh nim)
anonymous (uh NON uh muss)	pseudonym (SUE duh nim)
anonymously (uh NON uh muss lee)	synonym (SIN uh nim)

<u>Prefixes</u>
a—without
acro—tip
ant—opposite
hetero—different
homo—same
patr—father
pseudo—false
syn—together

<u>Suffixes</u>
ly—adverbial ending, telling
   in what manner something
   is done
ity—state of

Many authors write under a "pen name" or pseudonym.

false name
  pseudo—false
  onym—name

<u>Pseudonym</u> literally means _____.

<u>Calm</u> and <u>peaceful</u> mean almost the same thing; they

synonyms

are called _____. ("together words")

<u>Calm</u> and <u>troubled</u> are <u>antonyms</u>. That is, their

opposite
  ant—opposite
  onym—name

meanings are _____.

Organizations are often named so that their initials
spell a word that is easily pronounced. BART (Bay
Area Rapid Transit) and CORE (Congress of Racial
Equality) are examples. Because BART and CORE
are formed from the first letters (tips) of other words,

acronyms

they are called _____. ("tip words")

When a surname like Johnson is derived from the name of the father (Johnson = the son of John), it is called a patronym. <u>Patronym</u> literally means

father name
  patr—father
  onym—name

_____.

<u>Sea</u> and <u>see</u> are spelled differently and have different meanings, yet they are pronounced as though they were the same words. This characteristic allows

homonyms

them to be classified as _____.
("same words")

<u>Wind</u> (to twist) and <u>wind</u> (air in motion) are spelled the same but have different meanings. Because they are pronounced differently, they are classified as

different words

<u>heteronyms</u>, which means _____.

A letter without a name signed to it is an <u>anonymous</u>

without a name
  a—without
  onym—name

letter. It is literally "_____."

If you wished to donate to a charity without identifying yourself (without giving a name), you would do so in

anonymously

what manner? _____

When they travel, some movie stars simply put on dark glasses and hope that people who recognize them

anonymity

will respect their desire for _____.
(state of being without a name; being unidentified)

Self-Test

1. Mark Twain was the _____ used by one of America's greatest writers, Samuel Langhorne Clemens. (false name; pen name)

2. The threat came in the form of an <u>anonymous</u> phone call. The caller was: short of breath/unidentified/a policeman.

3. <u>Cite</u>, <u>sight</u>, and <u>site</u> are frequently confused because they are _____ _____. (the same words; words pronounced the same)

4. We ought to call our organization something like Society of Amateur Psychologists so that we could use the _____ SOAP.

5. <u>Bass</u> (a fish) and <u>bass</u> (a male voice) are _____.
(different words; words pronounced differently)

6. Mr. Worthington donated large sums of money to the college _____

    _____. (in a manner based on not giving his name)

7. Love and hate are _____. (opposite words)

8. Hate and dislike are _____. (together words; words
    with almost the same meaning)

9. Swenson (the son of Swen) is a _____. (surname
    based on the father's name)

10. The hotel staff did whatever they could to protect Mr. Rosenfeld's desire

    for _____. (lack of identification)

Answers to Self-Test

1. pseudonym 2. unidentified 3. homonyms 4. acronym 5. heteronyms
6. anonymously 7. antonyms 8. synonyms 9. patronym 10. anonymity

(16) PAN, all

Derivatives:

panacea (pan uh SEE uh) panoply (PAN uh plee)
Pan-American panorama (pan uh RAM uh)
panchromatic (pan kro MAT ik) pantheism (PAN thee izm)
pandemonium (pan duh MOAN pantheon (PAN thee ahn)
  ee um)

Other roots
cea—cure
chrom—color
demon—devil
orama—view
ply—arms
the—god

Suffixes
atic—marked by
ism—theory, practice; belief

all

The Pan-American Highway extends through _____
the countries that border the Pacific Ocean.

all colors
  pan—all
  chrom—color

Something that is panchromatic is sensitive to _____

_____.

Something supposedly able to cure all kinds of medical
or political problems is a panacea. Panacea means

cure-all
  pan—all
  cea—cure

_____. Patent medicines that

promise to cure a wide variety of ailments are

panaceas

_____. (They may not cure

anything at all; they make you feel good temporarily because they contain so much alcohol!) A political program that is offered as a cure for all kinds of so-

panacea   cial and economic problems is also a _____.

It is unwise for someone to yell "Fire!" in a crowded theatre for fear of creating pandemonium. When people panic, they behave as though what had been let

all the devils   loose? _____
  pan—all
  demon—devil

The Pantheon in Greece was a temple for all the gods. Today we extend the meaning to a building commemorating heroes. For example, the Baseball Hall of

pantheon   Fame is the _____ for baseball players.

What would someone mean if he said that around the next bend in the road there would be a panorama of

a complete or   the city? _____
unbroken view

To believe that God is identical with the universe and

pantheism   is all-embracing is to believe in _____.
(belief that everything that exists is God)

A knight who arrived on the field of battle in full panoply wore a complete suit of armor. Today when a prime minister appears in the full panoply of office,

he appears in robes   what do you think is meant? _____
or other special
clothing (from   _____
early days)

Self-Test

1. The company's profits soared when it first introduced _____ film for home cameras. (sensitive to all colors)

2. A guaranteed minimum income for every family may be a good thing, but it sounds suspiciously like a panacea, which means _____.

3. North American Indian tribes gather there once a year in their full panoply of paint and feathers. Panoply is _____.

4. Their concept of God is confusing to us: to them He is present everywhere, at all times. Their religious belief seems more like what we would call

_____. (belief that everything that exists is God)

5. Releasing the mouse on the tea table caused _____ at the Friday Afternoon Bridge Club. ("all the demons"; a wild uproar)

6. The fifty-foot-long mural was a panorama of the old days on the Mississippi River. A _panorama_ is _____.

7. The ancient Greek temple built to honor all the gods was called the _____ _____.

8. Games participated in by all the countries of the Americas would be called _____ games. ("all-American")

Answers to Self-Test

1. panchromatic 2. a cure-all 3. robes or other special clothing 4. pantheism
5. pandemonium 6. a wide or unbroken view 7. Pantheon 8. Pan-American

(17)   PATH, feeling, suffering, disease

Derivatives:

antipathy (ann TIP uh thee)	pathologist (puh THAHL uh just)
apathy (AP uh thee)	pathology (puh THAHL uh gee)
empathy (EM puh thee)	pathos (PAY thahss)
osteopath (OSS tee uh path)	psychopath (SEYE koe path)
pathetic (puh THET ik)	sympathy (SIM puh thee)

Prefixes	Other roots	Suffixes
a—without	logy—study of	ic—marked by
anti—against	osteo—bone	ist—one who
em—inside, within	psycho—mind	y—act of, quality of,
sym—with, together		capacity of

act of
feeling with
  sym—with
  path—feeling

sympathy

Your ability to be moved by another person's hurts is called _sympathy_, which literally means _____. Sympathy is the capacity to share someone else's suffering. You would express _____ to a friend who had lost a loved one.

empathy
  em—inside
  path—feeling

A more complete identification with another's feelings is called _____. (act of being inside the feeling) Empathy is imaginative identification with someone else's feelings, ideas, or motives. For example, a baby nursing at its mother's breast may react with a stomach upset if the mother is frightened. Or a spectator may become so identified with a boxer that he himself reacts bodily to blows that hit the boxer.

Mr. Jones was quickly aware of Joan's <u>antipathy</u>.

dislike

Does Joan like or dislike Mr. Jones? _____
You can prove your answer by knowing that antipathy

feeling against
  anti—against
  path—feeling

means literally "a state of _____."

No one could understand John's <u>apathy</u> about his family's troubles. Did John appear interested or did he

unconcerned

seem unconcerned? _____
You can prove your answer by knowing that <u>apathy</u>

without feeling
  a—without
  path—feeling

means literally "a state of being _____

_____."

One of the meanings of <u>path</u> is "suffering." You can see how closely allied this is to the idea of "feeling."

suffering

A <u>pathetic</u>-looking person appears to be _____

_____, and he therefore arouses in us a feeling of pity.

When this feeling of pity is aroused in speech, writing, art, or music, it is given the name <u>pathos</u>. For example, Shakespeare's serious plays present us with the spectacle of good men suffering and call forth our

pathos

compassion. They contain the quality of _____.

<u>Path</u> also means "disease." The study of unhealthy conditions and processes caused by disease is called

pathology
  path—disease
  logy—study of

_____.

Tissue that is suspected of being cancerous should be

pathologist

examined by a _____. (one who studies diseases, especially those leading to death)

An <u>osteopath</u> treats diseases by manipulating the

bones
  osteo—bones
  path—disease

_____ and muscles.

If you say that someone is neurotic, you mean he is too nervous; but if you say that someone is a <u>psycho-</u>

mind
  psycho—mind
  path—disease

<u>path</u>, you mean he has a disease of the _____.
A <u>psychopath</u> has a mental condition bordering on insanity.

Self-Test

1. After conventional methods of treatment did not help his hip injury, he consulted a(n) _____. (one who manipulates the bones and muscles)

2. When sympathy turns into the stronger feeling of empathy, a therapist can begin to see the world from the patient's point of view. Empathy means

   _____.

3. Accounts of witnesses indicate that the killer may be a psychopath. This means that the killer: has a diseased mind/is an adolescent/is very religious.

4. She looked so _____ standing out there in the pouring rain that I asked her to come in and dry herself by the fire. (marked by suffering)

5. The study of abnormalities of the body, particularly those brought on by disease, is called _____. ("study of disease")

6. I am not worth bothering about; save your _____. (act of sharing or "feeling with" someone else's suffering)

7. Prolonged malnutrition had produced in the prisoners a state of apathy, which is a condition of being _____.

8. Dr. Throckmorton's diagnosis was confirmed by the hospital pathologist. A pathologist is _____.

9. The biography of Queen Victoria written by Cecil Woodham-Smith contains more _____ than earlier versions. (feeling of pity)

10. Mr. Hogarty began to help her and to explain things to her, and Jeanette felt her original antipathy gradually melting away. Antipathy means

    _____.

Answers to Self-Test

1. osteopath 2. being inside the feeling; identifying with someone 3. has a diseased mind 4. pathetic 5. pathology 6. sympathy 7. without feeling 8. one who studies abnormalities brought on by disease 9. pathos 10. dislike; feeling against

PHIL, love

Derivatives:

Anglophile (ANG lo file)   philatelist (fuh LAT uh lust)
bibliophile (BIB lee uh file)   philharmonic (fill har MON ik)
Francophile (FRANK oh file)   philosopher (fuh LOSS uh fer)
Philadelphia (fill uh DELL fee uh) philter, philtre (FILL ter)
philanderer (fuh LAN der er)

Other roots	Suffixes
adelph—brother	e—one who
bibl—book	er—one who, that which
harmonia—music	ic—marked by
soph—wisdom	ist—one who

If soph means "wisdom," one who loves wisdom and

philosopher
  phil—love
  soph—wisdom

searches for it is a _____.

A philharmonic society is formed by people who

love

_____ music.

one who loves books   What is a bibliophile? _____

a loving man   A philanderer is what kind of man? _____

_____

The problem is that he makes love to women without
having serious intentions.

A philter (philtre) is a drug or potion used to make a

love   person fall in _____.

If an Anglophile is a person who loves all aspects of

**a person who loves
all aspects of the
French culture**

the English culture, what is a Francophile? _____

_____

If adelph means "brother," what famous American
city has a name that means "brotherly love"?

Philadelphia

_____

The root ately originally signified a stamp showing
that a tax had been paid. Today a person who likes

philatelist   to collect and study stamps is called a _____

_____.

Self-Test

1. Calling a man a Don Juan is virtually the same as calling him a philanderer. What is a <u>philanderer</u>? _____

_____

2. Jason has carefully saved every book he has read since childhood—the mark of a _____. (booklover)

3. Like all _____, he dreamed of saving enough money to live in Paris for a year. (lovers of French culture)

4. The young prince was always reading, questioning his tutors, and embarrassing his father with questions about honor and justice. The old king shook his head sadly and admitted to himself that the next king would no doubt be a philosopher. A <u>philosopher</u> is one who _____.

5. Because the community was so far removed from a large urban center, Mr. Bowles suggested that all of us music lovers form our own _____ _____ society. (marked by love of harmony)

6. The old gypsy swore she had a <u>philter</u> that, when added to a man's drink, would cause him to do what? _____

7. My son, who encourages me to bring home from the office all the discarded envelopes, is a philatelist. What is a <u>philatelist</u>? _____

8. "The Spirit of '76" is the theme of the celebration to be held in _____ _____. (city of brotherly love)

Answers to Self-Test

1. someone who makes love without serious intentions 2. bibliophile
3. Francophiles 4. loves wisdom 5. philharmonic 6. fall in love 7. stamp-lover 8. Philadelphia

(19) POD, PED foot   PED, child

Derivatives:
biped (BEYE ped)   pediatrician (PEED ee uh TRISH un)
centipede (SENT uh peed)   pedagogue (PED uh gog)
millipede (MILL uh peed)   pedagogy (PED uh go gee)
pedal (PED uhl)
pedestal (PED us tuhl)
podiatrist (poe DEYE uh trist)
quadruped (QUAD rue ped)
tripod (TREYE pod)

Prefixes	Other roots	Suffixes
bi—two	agogy—leading	cian—one who
tri—three		ist—one who
quadr—four		y—act of
cent—hundred		
mill—thousand		

A <u>tripod</u> is a stand used to hold a camera steady.

three
  tri—three
  pod—foot

How many legs does the tripod have? _____

Man walks erect on two feet; he is therefore classi-

biped

fied as a _____. The four-legged horse

quadruped

he rides is a _____.

A <u>centipede</u> is an insect with many pairs of legs.

100

How many legs does it seem to have? _____
(Clue: how many cents are in a dollar?)

Another insect that seems to have a thousand feet is

millipede

a _____.

To make a car move faster, you press down on the

pedal

gas _____.

pedestal

A small statuette is often placed on a _____.
(foot stall; a base or foundation for a statue) If a
man places a woman on a pedestal he treats her as
though she were more godlike than human.

Ped also can mean "child," so <u>pedagogy</u> literally

"child leading"
  ped—child
  agogy—leading

means "_____." Pedagogy
means the art or science of teaching.

However, few teachers would care to be called a

pedagogue

_____ because the term has
come to mean a petty and narrow-minded person.

A <u>pediatrician</u> is one who treats children, while a

feet

<u>podiatrist</u> treats _____. For diseases
affecting children, you would go to see a

pediatrician

_____. For foot problems,

podiatrist

you would go to see a _____.

Self-Test

1. Their marriage faltered because John insisted on putting Lyne on a pedestal. What is a <u>pedestal</u>? _____

2. Most people in education feel that physical punishment is not a necessary component of pedagogy. What is <u>pedagogy</u>? _____

   _____

3. Be sure you're not close to Professor McGinty when you call him a

   _____. (petty, narrow-minded teacher)

4. Even though he showed a gruff exterior to children, Dr. Richards was a highly successful _____. (children's doctor)

5. Sheep, goats, and dogs are quadrupeds. <u>Quadrupeds</u> means _____

   _____.

6. Man is a _____. (two-legged creature)

7. The blisters on my feet became so painful I had to consult a _____

   _____. (foot doctor)

Answers to Self-Test

1. the base on which a statue stands 2. art of teaching or "child-leading"
3. pedagogue 4. pediatrician 5. four-legged creatures 6. biped 7. podiatrist

(20) POLY, many

Derivatives:
polyandry (pahl ee ANN dree)
polygraph (PAHL ee graff)
polylingual (pahl ee LING wuhl)
Polynesia (pahl uh NEEZ yuh)

polyphonic (pahl uh FAHN ik)
polysyllabic (pahl ee sil LAB ik)
polytechnic (pahl ee TEK nik)

<u>Other roots</u>
andr—husband, man
graph—record
ling—tongue,
    language
phon—sound (music)
tech—trade, skill

<u>Suffixes</u>
ic—marked by
y—practice of

What is meant by saying that a word is <u>polysyllabic</u>?

it is made up of
many syllables   _____

polylingual

If you speak two languages, you are <u>bilingual</u>. If you speak more than two, you are _____.

polyandry
  poly—many
  andr—husband

In some cultures a woman is allowed to have more than one husband at a time, a practice called _____ (many husbands). (Compare this term with <u>polygamy</u>, studied earlier, which is the practice of a man having multiple wives. <u>Polyandry</u> and <u>polygamy</u> are the appropriate terms when the culture approves of or allows multiple marriages; <u>bigamy</u> is restricted to a multiple marriage that is against the law.)

many islands

<u>Nes</u> means "island." The name Polynesia is given to a series of island groups scattered across the Pacific Ocean. <u>Polynesia</u> means _____.

many trades or
skills used in
industry

What would you expect to study at a <u>polytechnic</u> high school? _____

_____

polyphonic

What do we call music that has two or more voice parts, each having an independent melody but all harmonizing? _____
("many sounds")

polygraph

Because a lie detector records tracings of several different pulsations at the same time, it is known officially as a _____.
("many records")

Self-Test

1. The university choir specializes in singing polyphonic music. <u>Polyphonic</u> means _____.

2. To a beginning student of vocabulary, _____ words may seem difficult because they look like "big words." ("marked by many syllables")

3. Lucille grew up on military bases in Spain and West Germany; by age fifteen she was polylingual. <u>Polylingual</u> means _____

_____.

4. The people who settled Hawaii came from _____.
    (place of many islands)

5. Until almost the twentieth century some of the valley tribes practiced <u>polyandry</u>, which is the practice of _____.

6. The vacant building may be refurbished and reopened as a _____ _____ high school. (offering instruction in many trades and skills)

7. Baker teaches the art of lie detection to policemen and security agents from around the world. He has made many refinements in the use of the _____. ("many records")

Answers to Self-Test

1. many melodies or voice parts 2. polysyllabic 3. speaking many languages 4. Polynesia 5. having many husbands 6. polytechnic 7. polygraph

(21) POLIT, POLIS, city, citizen

Derivatives
 Acropolis (uh KROP uh liss)   Indianapolis (in dee un AP uh liss)
 cosmopolitan (koz muh PAHL uh ton)   metropolis (muh TROP uh liss)
 cosmopolite (koz MOP uh light)   politician (pahl uh TISH un)

Other roots	Suffixes
acro—high	an—belonging to
cosmo—world	ian—one who
metro—mother	ite—a person associated with

Indianapolis

The city of the Indians is _____.

The main city of a region is a metropolis. If <u>metro</u> means "mother," <u>metropolis</u> literally means

mother city

_____.

In ancient Athens the highest part of the city, strongly fortified, was known as the <u>Acropolis</u>, which means

high city
 acro—high
 polis—city

_____.

Every Greek citizen took an active part in the government of his city-state. In current use only someone who is in some way active in politics is called a

politician

_____, and the word is often used to mean a person who is active chiefly for his own sake or for his party, often at the expense of the general welfare.

"world citizen" cosmo—world polit—citizen	A <u>cosmopolite</u> is, literally, a "_____ _____." A person who feels at home in any part of the world is a <u>cosmopolite</u>. His interests and tastes are not narrowed to his own nation or
cosmopolitan	country; they are international or _____ _____. (belonging to a citizen of the world)

Self-Test

1. When John Fredericks returned from the gold fields, San Francisco had become a thriving _____. (main or mother city)

2. During the great age of seafaring, even small New England towns had about them a strongly cosmopolitan atmosphere. What does <u>cosmopolitan</u> mean here? _____

3. Our hotel room in Athens looked out toward the ruins of the <u>Acropolis</u>. The ruins were: on a river bank/ on a hilltop/underground tunnels.

4. Although Mr. Mayberry had traveled widely during his career, he still retained a great many local and national prejudices, and he could not by any stretch of the imagination be called a _____. (citizen of the world)

5. Indianapolis means "_____."

6. John David Cullens refers to himself as a "political leader"; I am inclined to think of him as just another _____. (a person active in politics)

Answers to Self-Test

1. metropolis 2. international; reflecting all parts of the world 3. on a hilltop
4. cosmopolite 5. "city of the Indians" 6. politician

(22)   PROTO, first, fundamental

Derivatives·
protagonist (pro TAG uh nist)
protocol (PRO tuh call)
protoplasm (PRO tuh plaz um)

prototype (PRO tuh type)
protozoa (pro tuh ZO uh)

Other roots
agon—struggle
plasm—something
        molded
zoa—animals

Suffixes
ist—one who

prototype   The first or primary <u>type</u> of anything is the _____

_____ .

protagonist   The main character in a play (or the central figure in a contest or conflict) is the one with whom we fundamentally identify. He is the hero or _____

_____ . (one who is first in the struggle)

"first animals"   Protozoa are one-celled creatures that belong to the most primitive section of the animal kingdom. If <u>zoa</u> means "animals," then <u>protozoa</u> means

" _____ ."

protoplasm   A watery or gelatinous substance considered the basis of physical life is called _____ .
(something molded first)

protocol   If you have just received an appointment as an officer or as an ambassador, you will quickly have to learn a system of etiquette known as _____ col, which in a sense means knowing who comes first in military or diplomatic circles.

Self-Test

1. The modern airplane has its _____ in the paper gliders made and thrown by school children. (first model or pattern)

2. Protocol required that the retiring general be given first consideration. <u>Protocol</u> is _____ .

3. Some form of _____ exists in almost every habitat, such as fresh or salt water, soil, sewage, and even the bodies of larger living animals. ("first animals")

4. In Ibsen's play <u>The Master Builder</u> the protagonist is an idealistic architect. <u>Protagonist</u> means _____ .

5. Nourishment passes up through a plant from cell to cell, which constitutes a single unit of _____ . (something molded first; the substance that is the basis for all life)

Answers to Self-Test

1. prototype 2. a system of etiquette 3. protozoa 4. hero or main character; "first in struggle" 5. protoplasm

23   PYR, fire

Derivatives:

pyre (PIRE)
Pyrex (PEYE rex)
pyrography (peye ROG ruh fee)
pyromania (peye roe MAIN ee uh)

pyromaniac (peye roe MAIN ee ak)
pyrophobia (peye roe FOBE ee uh)
pyrotechnics (peye ruh TEK niks)

Other roots
graph—writing
mania—madness
phobia—fear
technics—skill, craft

Suffixes
iac—one who
y—act of

Burning designs on wood, leather, etc. is an art

pyrography
 pyr—fire
 graph—writing
 y—act of

known as _____.

a fire used to
cremate a corpse

The body of a Viking hero was placed on a funeral

pyre. What does pyre mean in this context? _____

_____.

fireproof

Pyrex is a brand name for dishes or cooking utensils.
The name should tell you that these dishes are:
brightly colored/made of aluminum alloy/fireproof.

fire madness
 pyr—fire
 mania—madness

Pyromania literally means _____.
Pyromania is an irrational desire to set things on
fire. Whereas an arsonist sets a fire to get revenge

pyromaniac

or collect insurance money, a _____
often cannot explain his motives. (one who has fire
madness)

pyrotechnics

The making or display of fireworks is called _____

_____. ("fire crafts")

The meaning is often extended to other areas. For
example, a pianist's pyrotechnics would be his brilliant display of skill, especially in performing difficult music.

A person who has pyrophobia suffers abnormally from

fear of fire

_____.

Self-Test

1. A pyrophobiac and a _____ would make strange companions. (one with fire madness)

2. If we say that an opera singer is famous for her vocal <u>pyrotechnics</u>, what do we mean? _____

3. All of a warrior's most cherished belongings were placed near him on his funeral _____. (fire)

4. A morbid fear of fire is called _____.

5. Food cooked in a _____ casserole dish requires a slightly lower oven temperature. (brand name for fireproof)

6. Having already mastered two difficult crafts, Jonathon decided to take a course in <u>pyrography</u>, which is the art of _____ _____.

Answers to Self-Test

1. pyromaniac   2. that she sings with technique as brilliant as fireworks
3. pyre   4. pyrophobia   5. Pyrex   6. burning designs on wood or leather

(24)   SCOP, see

Derivatives:
    episcopal (ee PISS kuh puhl)   periscope (PEAR uh scope)
    horoscope (HORE uh scope)   scope (SCOPE)
    microscope (MEYE kruh scope)   stethoscope (STETH uh scope)
    microscopy (meye KROSS kuh pee)   telescope (TELL uh scope)

Prefixes	Other roots	Suffixes
epi—over	horo—hour	al—marked by
peri—around	micro—small	y—act of, science of
	stetho—chest	
	tele—far, distant	

microscope   Almost everyone knows that an instrument for seeing small things is a _____, but few people know that the science of using micro-

microscopy   scopes is called _____.

A submarine commander sends up a <u>periscope</u> when

see around   he wishes to _____ the surface
  peri—around   of the water.
  scope—see

telescope
  tele—far
  scope—see

An instrument that helps man see far-off objects such as planets and stars is a _____.

see the chest

Literally a <u>stethoscope</u> is an instrument used to _____, but in actuality it is used for hearing sounds in the chest.

scope

The part of an area or problem that the examiners decide to deal with, or "see," is called the _____ of the examination.

horoscope

A forecast which is supposed to "see" your future from the position of the stars at the <u>hour</u> of your birth is called your _____.

It is governed by overseers (bishops).
  epi—over
  scop—see

What does the word <u>episcopal</u> tell you about the structure of the Episcopal Church? _____

_____

Self-Test

1. In his study of viruses Dr. Danvers needs two assistants who are experts in tissue preparation and _____. (science of using microscopes)

2. During World War I soldiers spent a great deal of time in deep trenches. To observe military activity above ground in safety, it was common practice to use a <u>periscope</u>, which allowed them to _____.

3. The comet was visible only through a very powerful _____.

4. Mrs. Doolittle would not sign the contract because her horoscope warned against business activities on Tuesday. A <u>horoscope</u> is _____

_____.

5. Mr. Lewers told reporters it was outside the _____ of his investigation to fix the blame for the price-fixing. (area to be "seen")

6. Which church takes its name from the fact that it is governed by bishops?

_____

7. After a few preliminary questions about my illness, the doctor took out

his _____. (instrument for observing sounds in
the chest)

Answers to Self-Test

1. microscopy 2. see around 3. telescope 4. a forecast based on star
positions at the hour of birth 5. scope 6. Episcopal Church 7. stethoscope

(25) THE, god

Derivatives:

apotheosis (uh POTH ee uh sis)   theocratic (thee uh KRAT ik)
apotheosize (uh POTH ee uh size)   theocracy (thee OK ruh see)
atheism (AY thee izm)   theism (THEE izm)
monotheism (MON oh thee izm)   theology (thee AHL uh gee)
polytheism (PAHL ee thee izm)

Prefixes	Other roots	Suffixes
apo—change	cracy—rule by	ic—marked by
mono—one	logy—study of	ism—belief in
poly—many		osis—process

theism
  the—god
  ism—belief in

Belief in the existence of a god is called _____

_____.

a belief in the
existence of
one god

Monotheism is _____

_____.

a belief in the
existence of
many gods

Polytheism is _____

_____.

without a belief
in the existence
of a god or gods

Atheism is being _____

_____.

theology

The study of the nature of God and of His relations

to man and the universe is called _____

_____.

god

To apotheosize an athlete or a hero or a politician is

to treat him as though he were a _____.

apotheosis

rule by god

The process of raising a human being to the status of a god is called _____.

Theocracy means literally "_____

_____." The religious leaders and the political leaders were closely connected, and were sometimes the same people, in the early Puritan colonies in New England.

theocratic

These colonies had a _____ system of government.

Self-Test

1. In associating _____ with primitive people, he overlooked the Greeks and Romans, who were highly sophisticated yet prayed to many gods. (belief in many gods)

2. Some foreign observers point out that we Americans give our favorite athletes an uncritical adoration and reverence that amounts almost to apotheosis. What is apotheosis? _____

_____.

3. Most of the American colonies founded by religious groups tended to have a theocratic structure, at least in their formative years. Theocratic

structure means _____

_____.

4. Local political leaders appear to be trying to _____ the region's new congressman, "Honest Joe" Garrett. (make into a god)

5. Both Judaism and Christianity are based on _____. (belief in one god)

6. My two uncles continually argue about women, politics, and _____

_____. (study of the existence and nature of God)

7. During the time of the Spanish Inquisition a person accused of atheism would have feared for his life. Atheism is _____

_____.

<u>Answers to Self-Test</u>

1. polytheism 2. process of raising a man to a god 2. "rule by god," with religious and political leaders much the same 4. apotheosize 5. monotheism 6. theology 7. without belief in god

Now that you've mastered this chapter, you might enjoy a fresh look at the drawing that opens it on page 10.

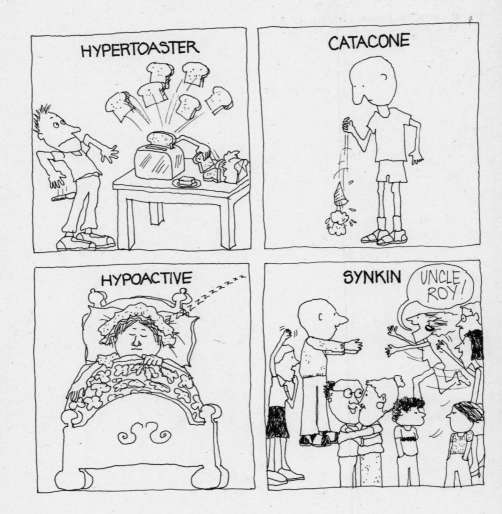

CHAPTER THREE
Greek Prefixes

 1 A-, AN-, without

Derivatives:

abyss (uh BISS)

adamant (AD uh munt)

amoral (ay MOR uhl)

anarchy (AN er kee)

anarchist (AN er kist)

anesthetize (uh NEZ thuh tize)

anemia (uh NEEM ee uh)

anemic (uh NEEM ik)

anodyne (AN uh dine)

apathetic (ap uh THET ik)

asymmetrical (ay sim MET ree kuhl)

atheism (AY thee izm)

atheist (AY thee ist)

atypical (ay TIP uh kuhl)

Roots	Suffixes
arch—rule, government	al—relating to
byss—bottom	ia—condition
damant—subdued	ism—condition
em—blood	ist—one who
esthet—sensation	ize—verb ending
odyne—pain	y—state of
path—feeling	
the—god	

You probably remember from an earlier unit that an atheist is a person without a belief in God. The word

a

is formed by adding the prefix _____ to theist. If theism means having a belief in God, then the word

atheism

meaning without a belief in God is _____ .
Damant means "being subdued." If you are adamant in refusing to accompany your parents on a long trip,

hold out

you: give in/hold out.   To be adamant means to be stubbornly opposed to or insistent upon something. If you are now beginning to see how the prefix a- functions, you will be able to choose the correct def- inition in the next item. To be apathetic about the

without feeling

fate of other human beings is to be: without feeling/ deeply concerned. Even if you did not recall from an earlier unit that path means "feeling," you could have chosen the right answer by knowing that a-

without

means _____.

If the left and right sides of a human face are without

asymmetrical

balance, then it is an _____ face. (not symmetrical)

To behave in typical fashion is to behave as most other people would in a given circumstance. Thousands of children laugh at the pranks of a clown; the one child that cries would be atypical. Whether it is a rock sample or a statistic, something that lies out-

atypical

side (without) the expected pattern is _____.

An act that is "not moral" is immoral. But if an act is committed without regard for the concept of right

amoral

and wrong, it is _____.

The prefix an- also means "without." It is a form of a- used before roots beginning with a vowel. Thus,

without pain
an—without
odyne—pain

anodyne literally means _____.
The medical term for pain-relievers is anodynes.

The term anemia literally means _____

without blood
an—without
em—blood

_____. Anemia normally means a person's blood is lacking in some way. In more general usage, a person who has no "life" or vitality is

anemic

said to be _____.

Why is a patient anesthetized before an operation?

so that he will
feel no sensation
of pain
an—without
esthet—sensation

_____.

You will recall that archy means "rule, government."

without rule or
government

Anarchy means _____.
Thus, a person who engages in destructive acts against a government in order to bring it down, to be without

anarchist

a government, is called an _____.

During an exploration of the North Pole, two scientists were lost when their sled fell into an abyss.

a bottomless hole

What is an abyss? _____.

abyss

The pit of hell is sometimes referred to as "the

_____." (bottomless pit) More
commonly, the word is used in a metaphorical sense
to emphasize or even exaggerate our feelings. In a
fit of despair Margaret says she feels she is standing
on the edge of an <u>abyss</u>. She means that she may fall

an immeasurably
hopeless or
wretched condition

into: a short period of illness/an immeasurably hopeless or wretched condition.

Self-Test

1. A blood test reveals that Mary suffers from a mild _____.
   (lack in the blood)

2. The surgeon nodded for his assistant to _____ the
   patient. (remove sensation from)

3. "Here," he said. "Take this <u>anodyne</u>." What will the anodyne do?

   _____

4. The professor dismissed John's example of prejudice as being uncharac-

   teristic and therefore _____. (outside the expected
   pattern)

5. The governor was <u>adamant</u> in his stand against the proposed legislation.
   The governor was: angry/incorrect/firm.

6. The speaker made a gloomy prediction that the nation would slide into an

   abyss of financial despair. <u>Abyss</u> means _____

   _____.

7. An architect who purposely designs buildings so that there is no obvious

   balance of parts is following the principle of _____
   design. (without symmetry)

8. Believing in neither right nor wrong, Hubert felt his acts could only be

   considered amoral, not immoral. <u>Amoral</u> means _____

   _____.

9. The tiny kingdom was threatened from the outside by a powerful army;

   from the inside, by increasing signs of _____. (state
   of being without a government; chaos in government)

10. Because he is so drained from his own long illness, Homer seems <u>apathetic</u>
    about his sister's accident. That is, he seems to be _____

    _____.

11. A person who is without belief in God is a(n) _____.

Answers to Self-Test

1. anemia 2. anesthetize 3. relieve or remove the pain 4. atypical 5. firm
6. without bottom; a bottomless pit 7. asymmetrical 8. without regard to
morality 9. anarchy 10. without feeling 11. atheist

② ANTI-, ANT-, against

Derivatives:
antibiotic (an tee beye AHT ik)
anticlimax (an tee KLEYE max)
antidote (AN tee dote)
antipathy (an TIP uh thee)
antisocial (an tee SO shuhl)
antiseptic (an tee SEP tik)

antitrust (an tee TRUST)
anti-American (an tee American)
anti-Christian (an tee Christian)
antagonist (an TAG uh nist)
Antarctic (ant ARK tik)

Roots
agon—struggle
bio—life
dote—poison
path—feeling

Suffixes
al—relating to
ic—relating to
ist—one who
y—state of being

Study these words carefully: antiwar, anti-aircraft.

anti

Both begin with the prefix _____. If you are

against

antiwar, you are _____ war; anti-

against

aircraft guns are used _____ aircraft.

If a person dislikes social occasions such as parties and does not seem to desire companionship, he is

antisocial

probably _____. ("against social")

At some time or other almost everyone has taken a pill or had an injection that helps him fight an infection or virus. A medicine that fights a "living" virus

antibiotic
anti—against
bio—life

is commonly known as an _____.

An antidote is a substance that works _____

against poison
anti—against
dote—poison

_____. The meaning can be extended to mean a remedy for any kind of evil.

A septic condition involves bacteria and decay. To prevent or retard the growth of bacteria, we can use

antiseptic

an _____.

against

Sympathy is a feeling together with someone; antipathy is a feeling _____ someone.
People we like call forth our sympathy at almost any
time. People we strongly dislike bring forth our

antipathy

_____ .

antitrust

Legislatures often pass laws to protect the general
public from large corporations or trusts that may attempt to corner the market on a product or use unfair

business practices. Such laws are called _____

_____ laws. (against trusts)

anticlimax

The _climax_ of a play occurs when the central conflict
is resolved. Usually this is also the highest point of
interest—for example, when the hero unmasks the
villain or defeats him. If a play continues to an event
much less important than what has gone before, then

that event is called an _____ .
("against climax")

anti-Christian

In the word anti-American the prefix is used with a
hyphen because it is joined to a proper noun, which
is of course capitalized. Write down the word you
would form to mean "against that which is Christian."

_____ .

Antarctic

The variant prefix ant- is sometimes used before
roots beginning with a vowel (antacid = ant + acid).
If the Arctic is located at the top of the Northern
Hemisphere, what do we call the similar region located opposite it, in the Southern Hemisphere? The

_____ .

antagonists
 agon—struggle
 ist—one who

it angers you (and
you oppose him)

Two people who fight against each other are opponents

or _____ .

If a friend's remark _antagonizes_ you, what does it

do? _____

_____

In the discussion of plays you will often encounter the
terms _protagonist_ and _antagonist_. These terms are
a carryover from athletic contests held in front of
Greek crowds. The _protagonist_ is the champion we
are rooting for; the _antagonist_ is the one who opposes
him. Thus in a play the _protagonist_ is the hero and
the _antagonist_ is the villain.

Self-Test

1. The dentist recommended that he gargle with a mouthwash containing a mild _____. (a substance that helps prevent decay)

2. Since the unfortunate quarterback had already been chewed out by his coach and teammates, his kid brother's ribbing came as an anticlimax to what had been a very dramatic day. An <u>anticlimax</u> is _____
   _____.

3. The two former friends, now _____, are doing their best to discredit each other politically. (opponents)

4. Janet's shaming laughter and her refusal to listen to his explanation produced in Fred a deep and unexpected antipathy. <u>Antipathy</u> means _____
   _____.

5. Charlotte's easy acceptance of him was a(n) _____ for the poisonous self-doubts that had crept into his mind. (remedy for an evil)

6. From Dick's behavior at the party it was difficult to tell whether he was _____ or just too tired to relate to anyone. ("against social")

7. Her fever began to be less pronounced a few hours after she took the antibiotic. What is an <u>antibiotic</u>? _____

Answers to Self-Test

1. antiseptic 2. an abrupt descent from the important to the trivial 3. antagonists 4. dislike; feeling against 5. antidote 6. antisocial 7. a medicine against infection or virus

(3) CATA-, down

Derivatives:
cataract (KAT uh rakt)
catacomb (KAT uh comb)
catapult (KAT uh puhlt)
cataclysm (KAT uh klizm)

cataclysmic (kat uh KLIZ mik)
catalog (KAT uh log)
catastrophe (kuh TASST ruh fee)
catalyst (KAT uh list)

Roots
act—dash
clys—wash
log—reasoning
lyst—break
pult—hurl
strophe—turn

Suffixes
ic—relating to

If you wished to see a list and brief description of the items sold by a mail order company, you would look at its catalog, in which the items are "spoken down"—that is, written down or listed. Catalog can also be used as a verb. What would be your task if you were to catalog the paintings of a famous artist?

to list and briefly describe them

During the period of their persecution by the Romans, the early Christians hid in the catacombs, which were galleries containing burial vaults. The prefix meaning enables you to determine that the catacombs were: aboveground/underground galleries.

underground

A violent storm causing great destruction is called a

cataclysm

_____. ("wash down") Such a storm lets loose tremendous quantities of water that "wash down" the countryside, changing the face of the land. Even though they do not involve water, other violent upheavals of nature, such as earthquakes, can also

cataclysmic

be called _____ occurrences.

In ancient times a machine used to hurl rocks against a wall or fortification was called a catapult ("down hurler"). A rock that was being catapulted would rise steeply into the air, trace an arc, and then fall downward. Today catapult is most often used as a verb, retaining chiefly the idea of something shooting upward at great speed. If a singer is catapulted into

quickly

fame, he reaches fame very: quickly/slowly. This exemplifies how a word can gradually change, sometimes distorting, even reversing, its original meaning.

In a play or in real life, when a man's fortunes suddenly and dramatically undergo a complete "downturn,"

catastrophe

we say he has suffered a _____.

A cataract is the "dashing down" of water, as in a large waterfall. Steep rapids in a river and sudden

cataracts

torrents of rain can also be called _____

"dashing down"

because in both cases there is a heavy "_____

_____" or downpouring of water.

A cataract can also be a cloudiness of the eye that

"dashes down"

"_____" over the lens, blotting vision.

A catalyst is "that which breaks (things) down." A catalyst triggers a chemical reaction without itself

"break down"

being changed. When it is added to two other substances, it causes them to " _____

_____ " and react with each other.

Self-Test

1. The sudden and dramatic drop in the stock market was a _____
    for many small investors. ("downturn")

2. Cataracts of rain quickly flooded the busy intersection. In this context
    cataracts are _____.

3. The flood of 1933 was the state's worst _____.
    (a violent storm causing great destruction)

4. Senator Johnson was catapulted into prominence when he published a book
    outlining the need for a third political party. How soon did he reach
    prominence? _____

5. If you were camping outdoors and the weatherman had predicted a storm
    of cataclysmic proportions, why would you be worried? _____

    _____

6. To escape the pursuing Romans, Rubus and his family hid in the _____
    _____. (underground galleries containing
    burial vaults)

7. The sodium chloride was a simple _____ that allowed
    the other two substances to interact freely. ("that which breaks down")

Answers to Self-Test

1. catastrophe 2. heavy downpourings of water 3. cataclysm 4. very quickly
5. because the storm would be violent and destructive 6. catacombs 7. catalyst

(4)   DIA-, across, through, thoroughly

Derivatives·
  diagnose (deye ugh NOSE)
  diameter (deye AM uh ture)
  diarrhea (deye uh RHEE uh)
  diaphanous (deye AFF uh nuss)
  diaphragm (DEYE uh fram)

  dialog (DEYE uh log)
  diagonal (deye AG uh nuhl)
  diadem (DEYE uh dem)
  diathermy (DEYE uh therm ee)

Roots
gon—corner
gnose—know
log—speech
meter—measure
phan—clear
phragm—fenced
rrhea—flow
therm—heat

Suffixes
al—marked by
ous—marked by
y—process

If <u>gon</u> means "corner," what kind of line is drawn across a square from one corner to the opposite

diagonal
  dia—across
  gon—corner

corner? A _____ line.

"across measure"
  dia—across
  meter—measure

If <u>meter</u> means "measure," <u>diameter</u> literally means "_____." In a circle, the diameter is a straight line passing from one side to the other giving the measure across the circle.

dialog

If <u>log</u> means "words about or speech," what do we call a discussion between two people, as in a play?

_____

know thoroughly
  dia—thoroughly
  gnose—know

A doctor examines a patient in order to <u>diagnose</u> an illness. He makes a careful study of the symptoms to find out what disease a person has. This current meaning is implied in the original meaning of <u>diagnose</u>, "to _____."

heat
  dia—through
  therm—heat

In the medical treatment called <u>diathermy</u>, what is sent through the body tissues? _____

diarrhea

What term is applied to an excessive discharge from the intestines ("a flowing through")? _____

diaphragm

What term means "fenced across" and denotes a body partition separating the chest from the abdominal cavities? _____

dia—across

A king wears a crown as a badge of royalty. In early days it took the form of a headband called a <u>diadem</u>. What part of the word <u>diadem</u> tells you it was worn bound about or across the head? _____

A dress made of <u>diaphanous</u> material would be so fine-textured or sheer that it would permit seeing

through   _____ .

  dia—through

Self-Test

1. A heating pad is one simple home device for administering _____

_____ . (heat through)

2. A stripper or exotic dancer might prefer to wear a costume that is nearly <u>diaphanous</u>. Such a costume would be: made of beads/a "see-through" gown/wash and wear.

3. Diarrhea is often a symptom of influenza ("flu"). What is <u>diarrhea</u>?

_____

4. Singers must sometimes practice breathing exercises to strengthen the

muscles of the _____ . (A body partition separating the chest from the abdominal cavities)

5. The Indian chieftain wore a headband so splendidly crafted it might have

been a king's _____ .

6. The editor drew a <u>diagonal</u> line across the page that was to be omitted

from the manuscript. How was the line drawn on the page? _____

_____

7. Lennie was examined by four specialists before one of them was able to

_____ his ailment. ("know thoroughly")

Answers to Self-Test

1. diathermy 2. a "see-through" gown 3. flowing through; an excessive discharge from the intestines 4. diaphragm 5. diadem 6. across the page from corner to corner 7. diagnose

(5)   EPI-, on, upon

Derivatives:

epidermis (ep uh DERM iss)	epitaph (EP uh taff)
epigram (EP uh gram)	epithet (EP uh thet)
epilepsy (EP uh lep see)	epitome (ee PIT uh mee)
epilogue (EP uh log)	epitomize (ee PIT uh mize)

Roots
dermis—skin
gram—writing
lepsy—take or seize
logy—speech
taph—tomb
thet—put
tome—cut short

Suffixes
ize—verb ending

on the skin
  epi—on
  dermis—skin

Epidermis literally means _____.
The epidermis is actually the outermost layer of skin on the body.

epilepsy

A nervous disorder in which the victim is seized or taken on by fits is called _____.

epigram

An epigram is a brief, witty comment on a single subject. It can be written or spoken; it is "quotable"; and it often contains a surprising turn of thought. For example, "All men are created equal, but some are more equal than others," is an _____.

"on put" or
put on
  epi—on
  thet—put

Thet means "put," so epithet means _____
_____.
If you hurl epithets at someone, you put abusive names on him (racist, male chauvinist pig).

speech on
  epi—on
  logue—speech

A play or television series like "The FBI" begins with a prologue (a "speech before"), proceeds through several acts, and ends with an epilogue, which is literally a _____. The epilogue is a final speech or commentary on what happened earlier.

on or upon a
tombstone

The word epitaph breaks down into epi- + taph (tomb) and means the inscription where? _____

epitaph

epitomize

_____. In one sense the word epitomize breaks down into epi- + tomize ("to cut short") and means to summarize briefly what was most typical or ideal: "Here lies John Thompson— kind husband, loving father, good citizen." In composing an _____ (inscription on a tombstone), someone tries to _____ (summarize briefly) the life or character of a deceased person.

to summarize or embody	Bob's experience <u>epitomizes</u> what happens to a freshman in a large university. Here <u>epitomize</u> means: to summarize or embody/to be one among many.
an ideal representation of patience	If Mr. Jones is the <u>epitome</u> of patience, he is: an ideal representation of patience/a bad example of patience.

Self-Test

1. "Backslider" and "draft-dodger" could be used as epithets. An <u>epithet</u> is _____.

2. His _____ read simply, "He loved God and his fellow man." (tombstone inscription)

3. In the epilogue of the play the father states that he never really understood his two sons. The <u>epilogue</u> comes: before the play/between the acts/at the end of the play.

4. Writing about political corruption, a reporter says, "Dishonesty is not a virtue, but it might as well be." He is using a(n) _____. (a short, witty remark)

5. Mr. Carruthers epitomized everything Sue liked in a boss. <u>Epitomized</u> means _____.

6. Man is still a creature of the sea, able to leave it only because, from birth to death, he lives in the water-filled space suit formed by his _____. (outermost layer of skin)

Answers to Self-Test

1. an abusive name "put on" someone 2. epitaph 3. at the end of the play
4. epigram 5. summarized the typical or ideal 6. epidermis

(6)   EU-, good, pleasant

Derivatives:
eugenics (yoo GEN iks)
eulogize (YOOL uh gize)
eulogy (YOOL uh gee)
eupepsia (yoo PEP see uh)
euphemism (YOOF uh mizm)
euphemistically (yoof uh MIST ik lee)

euphonious (yoo PHONE ee us)
euphony (YOO fun ee)
euphoria (yoo FORE ee uh)
euphoric (yoo FORE ik)
euthanasia (yoo thuh NAY zhuh)

Roots
gen—race
logy—speech
peps—stomach
phem—statement
        (speech)
phon—sound
phor—bring
thanas—death

Suffixes
ia—act of
ic—marked by
ically—adverb ending
ism—property of
ize—verb ending
ous—marked by
y—property of

One of the meanings of <u>logos</u> is "speech." If a man

He is praised;
good things are
said about him.
  eu—pleasant
  log—speech

is <u>eulogized</u> at his funeral, what do we mean? ____

_____

A speech delivered in praise of someone who has died

eulogy

or is retiring or is being honored is a _____.

Mercy killing—that is, giving an easy death to someone in great suffering—is called <u>euthanasia</u>, which

good or pleasant

literally means "_____death."

If <u>phon</u> means "sound," which derivative means good

euphony
  eu—pleasant
  phon—sound

or pleasant sound? _____

What kind of voice produces pleasant or melodious

euphonious

sounds? a(n) _____ voice

Which derivative denotes the science of improving the

eugenics

genetic characteristics of the human race? _____

You ask your chemistry professor how you did on the
last test. He knows you flunked, but to spare your
feelings he says instead, "You could have done better." Like all of us at some time or other, he is us-

good or pleasant

ing a <u>euphemism</u>—a _____
statement instead of a harsh one. On occasion you
may resent it if you wish a blunt, direct answer and

euphemistically

someone responds to you _____.
(pleasantly but indirectly)

The prefix <u>eu-</u> indicates that <u>euphoria</u> is an intense

pleasantness,
well-being

and sometimes abnormal feeling of _____

_____. Some people drink or re-

euphoric   sort to drugs to bring on a _____ state (marked by a feeling of well-being)

If dyspepsia is bad digestion, which derivative indi-

eupepsia   cates good digestion? _____

Self-Test

1. The little band of pioneers huddled together in the cold while the parson delivered a brief _____ over Buck's grave. (praising speech)

2. The parson hurried over Buck's hard drinking by referring to it _____ _____ as "Buck's one little weakness." (using a pleasant statement rather than a harsh one)

3. If a doctor withdraws life-support systems from an incurable, desperately ill person, can that act be called euthanasia? <u>Euthanasia</u> means _____ _____.

4. The medicine given him by the Indian guide not only took away the pain but also brought on an otherwise unexplainable _____. (exaggerated feeling of well-being)

5. The studio felt that Doris Day was a more <u>euphonious</u> name than Doris Dinglehoffer. That is, "Doris Day" sounded more _____.

6. Hitler readily embraced eugenics as a means of creating a German super-race. <u>Eugenics</u> is the science of _____.

7. The opposite of <u>dyspepsia</u> (bad digestion) is _____.

Answers to Self-Test
1. eulogy 2. euphemistically 3. act of giving someone a quick, painless death; mercy killing 4. euphoria 5. pleasant 6. improving genetic characteristics of humans 7. eupepsia

(7)   EC-, out, outside

Derivatives:

appendectomy (appen DECK tuh mee)	eclipse (ee KLIPS)
eccentric (ek SEN trik)	ecstasy (EK stuh see)
eccentricity (ek sen TRISS uh tee)	ecstatic (ek STAT ik)
eclectic (ek LEK tik)	ecstatically (ek STAT ik lee)
ecclesiastic (ik kleez ee ASS tik)	eczema (EK zuh muh)
ecclesiastical (ik kleez ee ASS tuh kuhl)	mastectomy (mass TEK tuh mee)
	tonsillectomy (tahn sill LEK tuh mee)

Roots	Suffixes
centr—center	ic, ical—relating to, marked by
clesi—clergy	ically—adverb ending
lect—pick, choose	ity, y—act of, state of, property of
lipse—omit, blot	
mast—breast	
stas—put	
tom—cut	
zema—boil	

If <u>zema</u> means "boil," which derivative describes a condition in which sores seem to boil out of the skin?

eczema
  ec—out
  zema—boil

_____

When the moon passes between the earth and the sun and blots out the sun, we call this act an <u>eclipse</u>. What does <u>eclipse</u> mean when used as a verb, in this sentence: Jonathan easily eclipsed his sister as an

He blotted out
her importance.

entertainer. _____

Professor Barnes has an <u>eclectic</u> taste in music. If <u>lect</u> means "choose," does he like only one kind of

no

music—say, classical? _____ You answered correctly if you figured that eclectic taste is based on selecting, or picking out, from many different choices.

Originally <u>ecclesi</u> meant "to call forth (out)" and then came to mean an assembly of citizens or church. Today a clergyman or preacher can be called an

ecclesiastic

_____, and when we speak of <u>ecclesiastical</u> affairs, we mean affairs that pertain

the church or
the clergy

to _____.

"Eccentric Leaves Million to Cat." Why would this headline be of interest? Because it describes someone doing something very unusual or odd. <u>Eccentric</u>

outside

actions are _____ the center of usual human behavior. By the way, most of us have at

eccentricity

least one little oddity or _____.

Have you ever heard the expression "Beside himself with joy"? The derivative naming this high emotional

outside

state is ecstasy, which means standing _____ oneself. When he received the award, Mike was

ecstatic

_____. (adjective form) When

ecstatically

Martha received the necklace, she sighed _____ _____. (adverb form)

Many medical terms end in -ectomy ("act of cutting

appendectomy

out"). Removal of an appendix = _____;

tonsillectomy

of tonsils = _____; of

mastectomy

a breast ("mast") = _____.

Self-Test

1. Reverend Trumbull has accepted an invitation to be a featured speaker at an ecclesiastical conference in Midland. The conference will be attended by: religious leaders/athletic coaches/businessmen.

2. In the poem John tried to capture the _____ of his love for Mary. (high emotional state)

3. The cook thought I was _____ because I asked to have my fried eggs chilled in the refrigerator before they were served. (odd or very unusual)

4. His extensive collection of books—light and serious, ancient and modern, classical and popular, American and European—proved that his taste in reading was eclectic. What does eclectic mean? _____

_____

5. The skin eruptions are possibly an indication of _____. ("boil out")

6. Norma recovered from the mastectomy in a much quicker time than she thought possible. A mastectomy is _____.

Answers to Self-Test

1. religious leaders 2. ecstasy 3. eccentric 4. based on selecting the best from many sources 5. eczema 6. removal of a breast

⑧   HYPER-, over, excessive   HYPO-, under, less than

Derivatives:

hyperactive (heye per AK tive)
hyperbole (heye PERB uh lee)
hypercritical (heye per KRIT uh kuhl)
hypersensitive (heye per SENZ uh tive)

hypoactive (heye poe AK tive)
hypochondriac (heye poe KOND ree ak ak)
hypodermic (heye poe DERM ik)
hypothermia (heye poe THERM ee uh)
hypothesis (heye POTH uh sis)

Derivatives (continued):

hyperthermia (heye per THERM ee uh)

hypothetical (heye poe THET uh kuhl)

hyperthyroidism (heye per THEYE roid izm)

hypothyroidism (heye poe THEYE roid izm)

Roots
bol—throw
chondr—breastplate
derm—skin
therm—heat
thes—put

Suffixes
iac—one who
ia—condition
is—noun ending
ism—condition

hypersensitive
    hyper—over

An excessively sensitive person is _____

_____ .

overactive;
abnormally
restless and
fidgety

A hyperactive child is a child who is _____

_____ .

hypercritical

John criticizes his wife's clothing very severely. She probably thinks of him as being _____

_____ .

hyperbole

Hyperbole is an extreme statement made for effect. "Your hands are as cold as ice!" is an example of

_____ .

under
    hypo—under
    derm—skin

An injection cannot be given over the skin.

If derm means "skin," a hypodermic needle gives an injection _____ the skin. Perhaps you have heard someone say "hyperdermic" needle. Why would "hyperdermic" be incorrect? _____

_____ .

hypothyroidism

hyperthyroidism

hyperthermia

Hyper- and hypo- are used to describe many medical conditions. An insufficient production of thyroxin would be _____ thyroidism; an excessive production of thyroxin would be _____ .

Above-normal body temperature would be _____

thermia; below-normal temperature would be

hypothermia

_____ .

It was Charles Darwin's hypothesis that only the fittest of the species survive. Here hypothesis means

under

an explanation placed _____ the facts and thought likely to be a true explanation. (Like a theory, a hypothesis is an explanation that is not yet proved, merely assumed.) If in arguing someone cites a hypothetical example, he is using an illustra-

made up but having
the appearance of
truth

tion that is: real/made up but having the appearance of truth.

The ancient Greeks thought that melancholy was lo-cated under the cartilage of the breastplate (hypo + chondros). A person in physical or emotional pain was supposed to clutch his breastplate—or at least actors portrayed them as doing so. Today a person who suffers from imaginary ailments, who in effect clutches his breastplate too often and without genuine

hypochondriac

cause, is called a _____.

Self-Test

1.   To be hypoactive is to be _____.

2.   "My love is as deep as the ocean" is an example of hyperbole, which is

_____.

3.   Because I reported in to sick bay three times in two weeks, the captain

branded me as a hypochondriac. That is, he thought I was _____

_____.

4.   The doctor said the antibiotic could be given only as a _____

injection. (under the skin)

5.   For reasons of security, the space scientist said he would illustrate his

generalizations with the experience of two _____

astronauts. (made up but having the appearance of truth)

6.   A condition in which the body temperature is below normal is _____

_____.

Answers to Self-Test

1. less active than normal 2. overstatement for effect 3. a person with im-aginary ailments 4. hypodermic 5. hypothetical 6. hypothermia

(9)   PARA-, PAR-, alongside

Derivatives:
    parable (PEAR uh buhl)
    parallel (PEAR uh lell)
    paranoia (pear uh NOY yuh)
    paraphernalia (pear uh fer NAIL yuh)

    paraphrase (PEAR uh fraze)
    paraprofessional (pear uh pro FESS shun uhl)
    parasite (PEAR uh site)
    parody (PEAR uh dee)

Roots	Suffixes
allel—of one another	al—relating to
ble (bol)—throw	ia—things
noia—mind	
oide—song	
phernal—dowry	
phrase—say	
sitos—food	

alongside
  para—alongside

Parallel lines run _____ each other and are everywhere equidistant from each other.

alongside

A parasite lives beside and feeds on another plant or animal.   Literally parasite breaks down into para

a parasite

(_____) + sitos (food).   In anger, what might you call a sponging relative who makes no effort to support himself? _____

paraphrase

Phrase means "say."   If you cannot remember a quotation exactly, then you say it in your own words, or _____ it.   ("say alongside")

If par means "alongside" and oide means "song," which of the above derivatives would describe a nonsensical imitation of a serious piece of writing?

parody

_____

Today we say that someone with a mental derangement is out of his mind.   The Greek word for madness was paranoia—a state of being alongside one's mind.

para

Which part of the word means "alongside"? _____
It is worth noting that a person suffering from paranoia usually has delusions of being persecuted or else has delusions of grandeur.

alongside a professional

A paraprofessional is someone who works _____

_____.   A paraprofessional usually performs some professional duties under the supervision of a qualified professional, such as a doctor or teacher.

Jesus often taught the multitudes by using parables. The word parable originally meant a comparison,

alongside

and derives from para ("_____") + ble ("thrown"). A parable is a brief story that illustrates a moral or spiritual truth.

alongside

Paraphernalia originally meant "_____ the dowry" and was applied to the personal belongings a bride took along with her. Paraphernalia still means personal belongings, but more specifically it means equipment or materials for a special purpose. Thus, in packing for a camping trip, you would include a

paraphernalia

backpack, a tent, and other _____.
(equipment brought along)

Self-Test

1. The tree was slowly being destroyed by two different parasites. What is a parasite? _____

2. It took fully ten minutes for the photographer to transfer his _____
_____ from the trunk of my car to his wife's station wagon. (equipment associated with a particular activity)

3. The night club audience laughed uproariously at the comedian's parody of the famous poem "Trees." What is a parody? _____
_____

4. Frank has been hired as a _____ and will assist in the chem lab under the supervision of Dr. Connors. (someone who works alongside a professional)

5. Betty's grandfather had no doubt intended the story to be a _____, but we failed to find a moral in it. (a story illustrating a moral)

6. His distrust and suspicion of everyone around him led us to believe that he was suffering from _____. (a madness characterized by delusions of persecution)

7. I could not recall the quotation exactly so I had to _____ it.

8. Six streets near the center of town were converted to _____ parking. (side-by-side)

Answers to Self-Test

1. something feeding on another plant or animal 2. paraphernalia 3. a comic imitation of serious writing 4. paraprofessional 5. parable 6. paranoia 7. paraphrase 8. parallel

  PERI-, around, near

Derivatives:

pericardium (pear uh KARD ee um)   periphery (per IF er ee)
perigee (PEAR uh gee)   periphal (per IF er uhl)
perimeter (puh RIM uh ter)   periscope (PEAR uh skope)
peripatetic (pear uh puh TET ik)

Roots
card—heart
gee—earth
meter—measure
patet—walk
pher—carry
scope—see

Suffixes
al—relating to
ic—marked by
ium—that which
y—act of, result of

look around
  peri—around
  scope—look

A <u>periscope</u> is an instrument used in a submarine to _____ the surface of the ocean.

perimeter
  peri—around
  meter—measure

If you walk all the way around the top of a volcano, you trace out its outer measurement or _____
_____.

Someone who is shy may wish to remain at the outer edge of a crowd; he feels more secure on the periphery. What part of the word <u>periphery</u> tells us the

peri

person is <u>around</u> the edge of the crowd? _____

Why would you feel dissatisfied if a speaker had touched only on <u>peripheral</u> issues of a controversy?

he had missed
the main issues

Because _____.

<u>Peri-</u> can also mean "near." As the moon or a satellite revolves about the earth, it traces out an oval rather than a completely round pattern. When the moon is farthest from earth, it is at its <u>apogee</u>; when

perigee

nearest the earth, it is at its _____.

Aristotle was known as the <u>peripatetic</u> philosopher because he liked to walk around from place to place as he philosophized. What would it be appropriate to call a teacher who paced the floor incessantly while talking to a class? _____

a peripatetic teacher

If card means "heart," where would the membranous sac called the pericardium be located? _____

around the heart

_____

Self-Test

1. The _____ of the pond was nearly two thousand feet. ("measure around")

2. Dr. Murray's ideas are original and interesting, but I am frequently distracted by his peripatetic manner in front of an audience. Peripatetic means _____.

3. The committee members were in such disagreement they could decide only on _____ matters like printing some posters. (around the edge)

4. At its perigee the satellite will be visible to the naked eye, since at that time it will be only 157 miles from the earth. The perigee is its: nearest point/farthest point.

5. The membranous sac enclosing the heart is called the _____. ("around the heart")

Answers to Self-Test

1. perimeter 2. walking around 3. peripheral 4. nearest point 5. pericardium

(11)   SYN-, SYM-, SYL-, SYS-, together, with

Derivatives:

syllable (SILL uh buhl)

synonym (SIN uh nim)

syllogism (SILL uh jizm)

synopsis (sin OP sis)

sympathy (SIM puh thee)

syntax (SIN tax)

symposium (sim POSE ee um)

synthesis (SIN thuh sis)

synchronize (SIN krun ize)

system (SIS tum)

Roots	Suffixes
chron—time	ism—act of
lable—gather, take	ium—act of
log—reasoning	ize—verb ending
onym—name	sis—act of, process

Roots (continued)
op—eye
path—feeling
pos—drink
tax—arrange
tem—to cause to stand
thes—put

Suffixes
y—act of

The prefix syn- and its variants occur in many words that you already know. Words that mean approximately the same thing and can be used to define each other (for example, the words hurtful and injurious) are

synonyms

called _____. If you "feel with" another person who is having troubles, you project

sympathy

_____ for him. Letters are "gathered together" to form a sound called a

syllable

_____. Things are "caused to

system

stand together" to form a _____.

Because synonym, sympathy, syllable, and system are everyday words, you probably filled in the blanks without even thinking about the fact that you were using a different form for each one. Which form to use with which root is largely determined by what will sound best. Try saying "synlable," "symlable," or "syslable" and you will see for yourself.

Use the prefix syn- to complete the following sentence: The sergeant told his men to set their watches at the exact same time before they began their operation.

synchronize
  syn—together
  chron—time

That is, the sergeant told them to _____ their watches.

together

You are warned to watch your syntax; you are warned to be careful how you arrange words _____ to form a sentence, phrase, or clause.

An essay of five thousand words has been reduced to a one-paragraph synopsis. Literally, you are then

view together
  syn—together/op—view

a short summary

able to _____ its main ideas.

A good synonym for synopsis would thus be: a light sketch/a short summary.

Originally symposium meant "drinking together." Here is an example of more current usage: Local police officers will attend a two-day symposium on riot control.   What does <u>symposium</u> mean here?

getting together
to exchange ideas   _____

Here is a pattern of logic or reasoning commonly in
use:
    All mortals must die.
    John is mortal.
    Therefore, John must die.
If the first two statements (called premises) are true,
then the third statement (the conclusion) must also be
true.   This way of putting together ideas to arrive at

syllogism   a conclusion based on them is called a _____

_____.   ("reasoning together")
Now look at this pattern:
    All blondes are dumb.
    Mary is a blonde.
    Therefore, Mary is dumb.

syllogism   Right? No—wrong! The _____
contains a faulty premise, because it remains to be
proved that all blondes are dumb.

An analysis involves taking something apart into its
separate, smaller units.   A <u>synthesis</u> involves putting

together   things _____ into a meaningful
whole. You would make an analysis of a difficult essay in order to understand it better.   On the other

synthesis   hand, your philosophy of life is probably a _____
of concepts you have gleaned from a wide variety of
people, influences, and experiences.

Self-Test

1.   It never occurred to Jim and Helen, when they agreed to meet at eight

o'clock, that they ought to _____ their watches.
(set to the same time)

2.   The new remedial English course will cover syntax and basic composition.

What is <u>syntax</u>? _____

3.   Your _____ is incorrect because in your major
premise you assume that all neurotics have creative ability.   (pattern of
logic, with premises and conclusion)

4.   Dr. Markov's theory of personality is a _____ of
psychological ideas taken from Freud, Jung, Horney, and Sullivan.   (putting together)

5. The symposium on social planning is open to the public. A <u>symposium</u> is

    _____ .

6. If you write a <u>synopsis</u> of a play, you are writing: a parody of the play/
    a lengthy essay on some aspect of the play/a short summary of the main
    ideas and events.

<u>Answers to Self-Test</u>

1. synchronize 2. arrangement of words in sentences 3. syllogism 4. synthesis 5. meeting to exchange ideas 6. a short summary of the main ideas
and events

    Now, having mastered this chapter, it might be fun to take another look
at the illustration on page 62.

CHAPTER FOUR
Latin Roots

(1) ACT, AG, IG, do, drive, carry on, move

Derivatives:

activate (AK tuh vate)
actor (AK ter)
actuary (AK choo air ee)
agent (AY junt)
agitate (AJ uh tate)

agile (AJ uhl)
agility (uh JILL uh tee)
deactivate (dee AK tuh vate)
litigation (lit uh GAY shun)
navigator (NAV uh gay ter)

Prefixes
de—do the opposite
    of

Other roots
lit—lawsuit
nav—ship

Suffixes
ary—one who
ate—verb ending
ation—act of
ent—one who
ile—able to
ity—quality of
or—one who

actor

Since he is "one who moves" about the stage, a person who has a role in a play is called an _____.

In case of an automobile accident you would call your insurance agent. ("one who does"; one who does things for another person) Another word that literally means "one who does" is actuary, which refers to the person who figures rates and risks in an insurance business. Thus, to arrange insurance for your car,

agent

you would see an _____, while the person who calculates how much the company should

actuary

charge for insurance is an _____.

To get money back for damages to your car, you may find yourself involved in litigation. What is litigation? Enter your answer in the blank on the next page.

the act of carrying
on a lawsuit
  lit—law
  ig—carry on
  ation—act of

_____

Which derivative means literally "able to move" and is often used to describe cats because they move with

agile

such grace and ease? _____ In general,

agility

young people have more _____ than older people. (ability to move easily)

Washing machines clean clothes by moving them around in soapy water. Another way to say it is that

agitates

a washing machine _____ the clothes. (drives or moves) Agitated can also be applied to people. In the sentence, "After their argument he remained in an agitated state for hours," the word agitated would mean: busy/inactive/nervous or upset.

nervous
or upset

drives or moves
a ship

A navigator is literally a person who _____

_____.

Actually the navigator guides a ship from place to place. This meaning has been extended, so that a

navigator

person who guides a plane is also called a _____

_____.

At the beginning of the dyeing process, the foreman pulled a switch that activated the machine. What did

He put the machine
into operation

he do? _____

When a naval ship is no longer to be used, it is

It is taken out
of use

deactivated. What happens to the ship? _____

_____

Self-Test

1. I didn't think that my grandfather would have the _____ to perform rock-and-roll dance movements. (ability to move easily)

2. Their argument over the boundary line may lead to some very expensive, long-drawn-out litigation. Litigation is _____

_____

3. My insurance agent said that an _____ would have to determine the new rates. ("one who does")

4. Each ship of that size is assigned two <u>navigators</u>. What is a navigator's job? To _____.

5. Fifteen hundred people were put out of work when the war plant was _____. (taken out of use)

6. The mechanism can operate at full capacity from the moment it is activated. <u>Activate</u> means _____.

Answers to Self-Test

1. agility 2. the act of carrying on a lawsuit 3. actuary 4. guide the ship from place to place 5. deactivated 6. to put into use

(2)   AM, AMAT, love, loving

Derivatives:

amateur (AM uh ter)	amity (AY muh tee)
amatory (AM uh tore ee)	amorous (AM uh russ)
amiability (aim ee uh BILL uh tee)	amour (uh MORE)
amiable (AIM ee uh buhl)	

Suffixes
abil—able to
ity—quality of
ory—relating to
ous—marked by

love

amateur

An <u>amateur</u> participates in sports, hobbies, and the like out of _____ for the activity. A beginner is also called an _____.

amorous

People in the mood to make love are said to be _____. (marked by loving)

quality of loving;
friendliness
  am—love
  abil—able to
  ity—quality of

An occasional person needs a few drinks before he achieves amiability. What is <u>amiability</u>? _____

_____

amiable

Those who like other people and get along well with them are _____ people. (relating to loving or liking)

warm

<u>Amity</u> between nations would mean a: warm/cold relationship.

Casanova was not at all reluctant to discuss his

amatory   _____ adventures. (relating to
love-making)

A book that promises to tell you all about the life of
a famous actress says it will include her amours.

her love   What do you think is meant? _____
affairs

Self-Test

1. Susan's sometimes alarming frankness is balanced by her _____
    _____. (quality of loving or liking others)

2. "Spare me," he said. "Nothing is as boring to me as hearing about some-
    body else's _____." (love affairs)

3. Beneath her balcony stood six _____ young men, each
    ready to serenade her and declare his love. (in the mood to make love)

4. The amity existing between the countries could be destroyed if each con-
    tinues to violate the territorial rights of the other. Amity is _____

    _____.

5. Senator Ironton denied having had any amatory adventures in Paris. That
    is, he denied any: spy contacts/wrongdoing/lovemaking.

Answers to Self-Test

1. amiability 2. amours 3. amorous 4. a warm or friendly relationship
5. lovemaking

(3)   AQU, water

Derivatives:
    aquacade (AK wuh kade)   aquarium (uh QUARE ee um)
    aqualung (AK wuh lung)   aquatic (uh QUAT ik)
    aquamarine (AK wuh muh REEN) aqueous (AK wee us)
    aquaplane (AK wuh plane)   subaqueous (sub AK wee us)

Prefixes   Suffixes
sub—under   ous—characterized by being

water   Aquatic plants must have their roots in _____.

under the water   Subaqueous plants are plants that grow where? _____
  sub—under
  aqu—water   _____

aqualung

A device that allows divers to breath below water is

an _____. ("water lung")

water

If you are <u>aquaplaning</u> you are on a board being towed

swiftly across _____.

<u>Terra</u> means "land." Thus, a <u>terrarium</u> is a thing
or place relating to land—an enclosure for keeping
animals or plants indoors. What word would be used
for an enclosure used for fish and other creatures of

aquarium

the sea? _____

blue-green,
like sea water

If "marine" refers to the sea, the color <u>aquamarine</u>
would be: orange/purplish/blue-green.

aqueous

If a medicine is dissolved in water, it forms an

_____ solution. ("having the
quality of water") <u>Aqueous</u> applies only to chemical
solutions.

A form of entertainment called an <u>aquacade</u> originated
in Cleveland, Ohio, in 1937. It employed music and

water sports, such
as swimming and
diving

featured what kind of sports? _____

_____

Self-Test

1. These new blue-green fabrics are available in peacock blue, forest green,

and _____. (bluish-green like sea water)

2. Waterlilies and water hyacinths will be planted in the new _____

garden. (relating to water; needing a water environment)

3. The local swimming teams are planning to celebrate with an end-of-summer

aquacade. What is an <u>aquacade</u>? _____

4. What is the main characteristic of <u>subaqueous</u> plants? _____

_____

5. It is considered dangerous to dive to such depths without an _____

_____. ("water lung")

6. If chemical or medicine forms an <u>aqueous</u> solution, that means it is _____

_____.

7. Uncle Bert brought me a sea snail and some guppies for my new _____

_____ in the living room. (enclosure for water animals)

8. An illustration in the travel brochure featured three young people learning to aquaplane at Acapulco. What were they learning to do? _____

_____

Answers to Self-Test

1. aquamarine 2. aquatic 3. an entertainment featuring water sports 4. they live and grow under the surface of the water 5. aqualung 6. dissolved in water 7. aquarium 8. to be towed across water on a board

(4)   BENE, good

Derivatives:
      benediction (ben uh DIK shun)   benefit (BEN uh fit)
      benefaction (ben uh FAK shun)   benevolent (buh NEV uh lunt)
      benefactor (BEN uh fak ter)   benign (buh NINE)
      beneficiary (ben uh FISH ee air ee)

Other roots	Suffixes
dict—say, speak	ent—marked by
fact—do, make	ion—act of
fic—do, make	or—one who
fit—do, make	
ign—do, drive, carry on	
vol—will	

good
  bene—good
  fit—make

If you benefit someone else, you do him some _____

_____.

blesses them

A dying father gives his children a benediction. If dict means "speak," he: scolds them/blesses them.

good
  bene—good
  vol—will
  ent—marked by

A benevolent attitude is one that wishes _____. for others. A free clinic would be a benevolent organization.

You are your grandfather's favorite. In his will he has designated you as his chief beneficiary. You are

good

the one to whom he is going to do some _____.
In this case, you will receive part of the estate from your grandfather, who is your benefactor.

If factor means "one who does," what is a benefactor?

someone who
does good things

_____

You are grateful for his act of doing good—that is,

benefaction

for his _____.

A <u>malign</u> tumor continues to grow—literally, it does (<u>ig</u>) evil (<u>mal</u>). What kind of tumor does not continue

benign

to grow or cause further trouble? _____

Curiously, from the meaning "not harmful" the word <u>benign</u> has also come to mean "gentle" (a <u>benign</u> old man) or even "favorable" (a <u>benign</u> climate).

Self-Test

1. Mrs. Marshall and her friends consider their club to be a kind of _____

_____ society for helping orphans. (showing good will through actions)

2. Compared to the radical new governments that were replacing it, the old empire seemed mild—almost benign. <u>Benign</u> means _____

_____

3. Uncle Joe helped Ralph through college by giving him money and moral support. Uncle Joe is Ralph's _____. (one who does good)

4. Howard was a proud man, and he actually seemed to resent his father-in-law's frequent benefactions. A <u>benefaction</u> is _____.

5. Tom and Frank were ready to leave the church the minute the minister finished delivering the benediction. What is a <u>benediction</u>? _____

_____

6. The proceeds from the auction will be used to benefit homeless children. What does <u>benefit</u> mean? _____

7. Mrs. Madison's will was contested because she did not name any of her children as the _____ of her estate. (ones to whom something good is done; persons who receive money or property from a will)

Answers to Self-Test

1. benevolent 2. gentle; favorable; not harmful 3. benefactor 4. an act of doing good 5. a blessing (a prayer asking for God's blessing) 6. do good for 7. beneficiaries

5 CAP(T), CEPT, CIP, CEIV, CEIT, seize, take

Derivatives:

capacity (kuh PASS uh tee)
captivate (KAP tuh vate)
capture (KAP chure)
conceit (kun SEAT)
deceive (dee SEEVE)

incapacitate (in kuh PASS uh tate)
perception (per SEP shun)
receipt (ree SEAT)
recipient (ree SIP ee unt)

Prefixes	Suffixes
con—with, together	ate—verb ending
de—away	ent—one who
in—not	ity—ability to
re—back	ion—act of
per—thoroughly	

take or seize — If you <u>capture</u> someone's attention, you _____ it.

A <u>captivating</u> performance by an actress would be: interesting or charming/dull and boring.

interesting or charming

The abbreviation ESP stands for extra-sensory _____. (act of thoroughly seizing or taking an idea)

perception
per—thoroughly
cept—seize
ion—act of

A man has an illness that <u>incapacitates</u> him for a week. What does the illness do with respect to his job? _____

It makes him unable to take on his usual work.

The limit of the ability of a tank to hold gas or liquid is called its _____. (ability to take or seize something)

capacity

Mr. Bellamy is this year's recipient of the Good Neighbor Award. What does <u>recipient</u> mean? _____

A person who "takes back" or receives something (for his effort)

_____

_____

takes away
de—away
ceive—take

A friend deceives you. Literally, he "_____ _____" your faith in him.

receipt

Pay the cashier and take your _____ to the loading dock when you claim your merchandise. ("that which is taken back"; a written statement or ticket acknowledging that money has been paid for goods)

conceit   Laura Lee's personality is flawed by her _____

_____. (state of being taken with her-
self; high opinion of herself)

Self-Test

1. The injury to his back left Randall incapacitated for six weeks. <u>Incapaci-</u>
<u>tated</u> means _____.

2. Angelique's beauty and talent made her a _____ dancer.
(seizing the attention by some special charm)

3. Professor Dundee is a man of very quick _____.
(ability to seize an idea thoroughly)

4. The saleswoman forgot to give me a _____ for my
purchases. (something "taken back" to confirm payment for goods)

5. The recipients of the prizes all made brief speeches of appreciation. A
<u>recipient</u> is _____.

6. I can no longer trust her, since she once _____ me.
("took away" trust)

7. Most babies simply do not have the capacity to hold that much food at one
time. What does <u>capacity</u> mean? _____

8. Did you ever see such _____ in a man! (excessively
high opinion of oneself)

Answers to Self-Test

1. unable to take on his usual work 2. captivating 3. perception 4. receipt
5. one who receives or "takes back" 6. deceived 7. ability to take 8. conceit

(6)   CAPIT, head

Derivatives:
capital (KAP uh tuhl)
capitol (KAP uh tuhl)
captain (KAP tun)
decapitate (dee KAP uh tate)

decapitation (dee kap uh TAY shun)
per capita (per KAP uh tuh)
recapitulate (ree kuh PIT choo late)

<u>Prefixes</u>
de—off, down
per—by
re—again

person
  per—by
  capit—head

The per capita consumption of alcohol means the average amount consumed by each _____.

captain

The "head player" of a football team is its _____ _____. (Here the "i" is dropped from capit. You should be able to tell the difference between capt, "head," and capt, "seize," from the context or setting of a word.)

The capital of a state is its head city, which is the seat of the state government. The actual building housing the legislature is called the capitol. If a newspaperman reports a riot in the state capital,

the city

he means _____; if he reports earthquake damage to the state capitol, he means

the building
that houses
the legislature

_____.

A professor recapitulates his lecture of the previous day. He summarizes it briefly by repeating the

main points or
head ideas

_____.

In eighteenth-century France a common sentence for criminals was decapitation. What do you think decapitation is? _____

taking off the
head

Capital punishment is the head or most severe punishment that can be given—that is, death. Now complete this gruesome pun: In France the head punish-

decapitated

ment is to be _____ on the guillotine. (beheaded)

Self-Test

1. For the benefit of those who missed the first meeting, the chairman recapitulated the arguments against rezoning. What did the chairman do?

_____

2. Recent polls have indicated a dramatic increase in the _____ consumption of wine in the Western states. (by each person)

3. A group of pickets tried to bar the entrance to the state capitol. What does capitol refer to? _____

4. Senator Hopkins and his family moved to the state _____ last August. (head city)

5.   The French court sentenced the two criminals to death by <u>decapitation</u>.
     The criminals are to suffer what punishment? _____

     _____

<u>Answers to Self-Test</u>

1. reviewed the main points 2. per capita 3. the actual building housing a
legislature 4. capital 5. their heads are to be cut off

(7)   CARN, flesh

Derivatives:
 carnage (KAR nij)   carnivore (KAR nuh vore)
 carnal (KARN uhl)   carnivorous (kar NIV er us)
 carnation (kar NAY shun) incarnation (in kar NAY shun)
 carne (KAR nay)   reincarnation (ree in kar NAY shun)

Prefixes	Suffixes
in—in, into	age—result of
re—again	al—relating to
	ation—act of
	ous—relating to

	The carnation derives its original name from its pale
flesh	pink or _____ color.
flesh	Carnal desires are desires of the _____ .
	Chili con <u>carne</u> is a Mexican dish—literally, chili
flesh, or meat	with _____ .
	<u>Vor</u> means "eat." What do you think <u>carnivorous</u>
flesh-eating	means? _____ .
carnivores	Lions and tigers are flesh-eaters or _____
	_____ .
	A military commander who surveys the <u>carnage</u> after
have been killed or slaughtered	a battle looks at a great number of people who ____
	_____ .
	Another way to say that a young man represents an ideal is to say that he is the <u>incarnation</u> of the ideal
flesh	(the ideal put into _____).
	Some people believe that each of us is reborn into a succession of different bodies. The belief that we

reincarnation
  re—again
  in—into
  carn—flesh

are "made into flesh again" is called _____

_____ .

Self-Test

1. The sharp teeth of the animal showed that it was an ancient carnivore.
    What is a <u>carnivore</u>? _____

2. The Sons of Satan believe that their current leader is the _____
    of the devil. (act of being reborn)

3. The carnage of World War I brought about a wave of disillusionment and
    cynicism among young intellectuals both here and in Europe. <u>Carnage</u>
    refers to _____ .

4. The sight of her swaying, semi-nude body filled him with _____
    desire. (of the flesh)

5. Many pet owners are extremely upset when their cats catch birds, for-
    getting of course that cats are, after all, _____ .
    (flesh-eating)

6. We sat around the fireplace eating large bowls of chili con <u>carne</u>, which
    actually means "chili with _____ ."

Answers to Self-Test

1. flesh-eater 2. reincarnation 3. slaughter; killing 4. carnal 5. carnivorous 6. meat, or flesh

⑧   CEDE, CEED, CESS, go, move, yield

Derivatives:
  accede (ak SEED)
  cede (SEED)
  concede (kuhn SEED)
  exceed (ex SEED)
  intercede (in ter SEED)
  precede (pre SEED)
  precedent (PRESS uh dunt)

  proceed (pro SEED)
  recede (ree SEED)
  recession (ree SESS shun)
  secede (see SEED)
  succeed (suck SEED)
  unprecedented (un PRESS uh dent ud)

Prefixes
ac—to, toward
con—with
ex—outside
inter—between

pre—before
pro—forward
re—back

se—away from
suc—under
un—not

precede
  pre—before
  cede—go

Mr. Perkins will _____ Mrs. Dole on the speaker's platform. (go before)

receded
  re—back
  cede—move

After the flood the water quickly _____. (moved back)

The principal interceded and made peace between the

moved between
  inter—between
  cede—move

fighting boys. Interceded means _____

_____.

accede
  ac—toward
  cede—yield

Mary will usually _____ to a reasonable request. (yield toward, meaning to agree voluntarily)

conceded
  con—with
  cede—yield

Seeing that he could not possibly win, Sam _____

_____ the game to Fred. (yield with, meaning to be forced to agree)

secede
  se—away from
  cede—move

The South once tried to _____ from the Union. (move away from a group without the group's approval)

They proceeded with the work in the usual manner.

went forward

Proceeded means _____.

Each employee is rewarded with a small bonus if he

exceeds

_____ his quota of work for the month. (moves outside, goes beyond)

When prices increase and wages decrease, the economy enters a recession. Recession literally means

going back

_____.

When the Supreme Court makes a new decision, it

precedent

establishes a legal _____ that is followed by all the lower courts. (that which goes before and sets a model or pattern)

breaks the old
record

If a team wins an unprecedented number of its games, it: establishes the old record/breaks the old record.

Self-Test

1. Hester forced the minister to concede that he had been wrong. Concede

    means _____.

2. If Mr. Brooks accedes to the plan, he will provide the money. Accede

   means _____ .

3. People are now buying small cars in _____ numbers.
   (breaking the earlier record or pattern)

4. Economists will gather in Washington, D.C., to discuss methods of a-

   voiding another _____ . (act of moving backward)

5. Mr. Hill followed the old-fashioned social precedent of asking the men to
   join him in the library for a smoke after dinner. What is a precedent?

   _____

6. Biafra tried unsuccessfully to _____ from Nigeria.
   (leave a group without that group's approval)

7. It is wise not to _____ in a quarrel between a
   man and wife. (move between to bring about an agreement)

8. As he aged, his hairline receded. That is, he became: more handsome/
   hairier/balder.

9. This bill for repairs _____ your original estimate.
   (goes beyond)

10. After visiting the museum, we will _____ to a quaint
    little cafe for lunch. (move forward)

Answers to Self-Test

1. to admit or agree under pressure; "yield with" 2. to agree voluntarily; to
move toward 3. unprecedented 4. recession 5. custom; that which goes before and sets a model or pattern to be followed 6. secede 7. intercede
8. balder 9. exceeds 10. proceed

(9)   CLAM, CLAIM, cry, shout

Derivatives:

claimant (CLAIM unt)	exclamation (ex kluh MAY shun)
clamor (KLAM er)	proclaim (pro CLAIM)
clamorous (KLAM er us)	proclamation (prok luh MAY shun)
disclaim (dis CLAIM)	reclaim (ree CLAIM)
exclaim (eks CLAIM)	reclamation (rek luh MAY shun)

Prefixes	Suffixes
dis—apart	ant—one who
ex—out	ation—act of
pro—forward	
re—back	

The <u>clamor</u> of people in the street would be what

crying or shouting   kind of noise? _____

A college president is beset by a group of <u>clamorous</u>

loud and noisy   protesters. They are: disorganized and unruly/loud and noisy.

To claim something, you visualize yourself saying, "Hey, that's mine!" Nowadays the claiming more often takes the form of a ticket or paper with your name or identifying number written on it. When you surrender your luggage at an airline ticket counter, you are given a claim ticket in return. At the end of

reclaim   your trip you _____ your luggage.
  re—back   (claim again; "shout back")
  claim—cry

The Dutch have undertaken the <u>reclamation</u> of land that has been flooded by the North Sea. What are they

put it back into   attempting to do with the land? _____
productive use

_____

claimant   A claim check identifies you as the _____

_____. (one who makes a claim to something) If you read the fine print on the claim ticket, you will learn that the issuing company

disclaims   _____ responsibility ("cries
  dis—apart   itself apart from"; denies) beyond the limits set forth
  claim—cry   in the claim ticket.

Each year the President must proclaim one of our

shout forth   national holidays. <u>Proclaim</u> literally means _____
  pro—forward

_____.

proclamation   Thanksgiving Day is set by a presidential _____

_____. (act of shouting forward; public announcement)

Suddenly you run into an old friend you have not seen

exclaim   for years. You _____ (shout out),

exclamation   "How wonderful to see you again!" Your _____

_____ (act of crying or shouting out) is probably matched by one from your friend.

Self-Test

1. Tim's concentration was continually interrupted by the _____ of people enjoying a cocktail party in the patio next door. (noise made by shouting or loud talking)

2. According to the king's proclamation, the young woman whose foot fit the shoe would marry the prince. A proclamation is _____

_____.

3. He brought with him an original copy of the insurance policy to establish that he was indeed the _____. (one who claims)

4. Norman said he did not know about the mistake and disclaimed any responsibility for it. That is, he: denied/accepted/laughed at any responsibility.

5. What is the purpose of slum reclamation? _____

_____

6. The strongest _____ she ever uttered was "My, my." (act of shouting out; sharp or sudden utterance)

Answers to Self-Test

1. clamor 2. a public announcement; "a shouting forth" 3. claimant 4. denied; "cried apart" 5. to put a neighborhood or district back into productive use 6. exclamation

(10) CORP, body

Derivatives:
corporal (KORE per uhl)
corporeal (kore PORE ee uhl)
corps (KORE)
corpse (KORPSS)

corpus (KORE puhss)
corpuscle (KORE puss uhl)
corpulent (KORE pew luhnt)
incorporate (in KORE per ate)
incorporeal (in kore PORE ee uhl)

Prefixes
in—in or not

Suffixes
al—relating to
ate—verb ending
cle—noun ending (little thing)
ent—marked by
us—noun ending

body
corp—body

corps

The Marine Corps is a military _____. It usually consists of two or more divisions. The plural form is the same as the singular: The parade will be attended by members of all the military _____.

body
  corp—body
  us—noun ending
  cle—little thing

A <u>corpuscle</u> is a "little _____" or cell that floats in the blood or lymph. It carries oxygen and carbon dioxide, and it helps destroy disease germs.

body

<u>Corporal</u> punishment is inflicted on the: body/mind.

<u>Corporeal</u> things are "bodily" or material. They can be seen and touched. Things such as ghosts or spirits that can neither be seen nor touched are

incorporeal

_____. (not corporeal)

body

In law the body of a murdered person is called the

<u>corpus delicti</u>—"the _____ of the crime"—and is the fact that proves a crime has been committed.

corpulent

Fat or fleshy people would probably prefer to think of themselves as being _____.
It is a more clinical-sounding term and therefore less offensive to them.

corpus

A complete collection of writings, laws, and the like is called a _____. (Latin for <u>body</u>)

made into or put
into one body

Frank's various experiences with Alaskan wolves have been incorporated into a novel. What does <u>incorporate</u> mean here? _____

Self-Test

1. At last! Fashion styles for corpulent women. <u>Corpulent</u> means: skinny/ middle-aged/fat.

2. Your suggestion will be _____ into this new plan. (made part of; put into one body)

3. The spiritual medium promised the ladies that the room would be full of

_____ beings with whom only she could com- municate. (not having a physical body)

4. To say the least, Aunt Polly was generous with corporal punishment.

What is <u>corporal</u> punishment? _____

5. The marching bands were supplied by the Army and Navy and Marine

_____. (bodies)

6. Perry Mason asked the judge to dismiss the case unless the prosecuting attorney produced the corpus delicti. Here <u>corpus</u> refers to _____

_____ .

7. That short story should certainly be featured in the Hemingway _____

_____ . (body; collection of writings)

8. The blood test revealed that I am low in white corpuscles. What are <u>cor-puscles</u>? _____

Answers to Self-Test

1. fat 3. incorporated 3. incorporeal 4. punishment inflicted on the body
5. Corps 6. the body (of the murdered person) 7. corpus 8. "little bodies";
cells that help fight disease germs

(11) CLUD, CLUS, CLOIS, CLAUS, shut, close

Derivatives:

claustrophobia (klaus truh FOBE ee uh)
cloister (KLOY ster)
exclude (eks KLUDE)
include (in KLUDE)

malocclusion (mal uh KLUZE shun)
preclude (pre KLUDE)
recluse (REK loose)
seclude (see KLUDE)

Prefixes	Other roots	Suffixes
ex—out	phobia—fear	ion—act of
in—in	mal—bad	
oc—against		
pre—before		
re—back		
se—away		

include
 in—in
 clud—shut

Our plans also _____ you. (shut in; enclose)

excluded
 ex—out
 clud—shut

Twenty years ago automobiles were _____ from the island. (shut out)

They built their cabin in a <u>secluded</u> spot. What kind

shut away;
isolated

of spot was it? _____

precluded

A lack of money _____ the possibility of their taking a pleasure cruise this year. (shut before; prevented ahead of time)

someone "shut
back" from
public view

Emily Dickinson, famous American poet, preferred
to live as a recluse. What is a <u>recluse</u>? _____

_____

claustrophobia

Sailors who suffer from _____
are unsuited to submarine duty. (a phobia about
closed places)

The disillusioned princess spent the rest of her life
in a religious <u>cloister</u>. What kind of place do you think

a place shut off
from the world

a <u>cloister</u> is? _____

Hilda's teeth do not shut against each other properly.

malocclusion

Her problem is known as _____.
("bad closing")

Self-Test

1. A busy schedule of activities in October will _____ our
attending the folk dance festival. (prevent ahead of time)

2. For nearly six years Hawthorne seldom left his room, and many of his
relatives and friends thought he had become a _____ for life.
(person who shuts himself back from the world)

3. She dislikes riding in elevators because she is subject to <u>claustrophobia</u>,
which is _____.

4. What kind of dental problem is <u>malocclusion</u>? _____

_____

5. The young lovers often met in a _____ part of the park.
(isolated)

6. Both a monastery and a convent would be examples of a _____
_____. (place shut off from the world)

Answers to Self-Test

1. preclude 2. recluse 3. fear of being shut in 4. The teeth do not shut
against each other properly; there is a poor "bite." 5. secluded 6. cloister

(12)   CRED, believe

Derivatives:
     credence (KREED unce)   creed (KREED)
     credible (KRED uh buhl)   incredible (in KRED uh buhl)

Derivatives (continued):
    creditable (KRED uh tuh buhl)   incredulity (in kruh DUEL uh tee)
    credulous (KREJ uh luss)   incredulous (in KREJ uh luss)

Prefixes
in—not

Suffixes
able—able to
ible—able to
ity—state of
ous—marked by

Whether it is religious, political, or personal, a
creed is a statement of the principles or fundamentals

believes

someone _____.

John gives us a long story to explain his lateness. If

credible
  cred—believe
  ible—able

his story is believable, we say it is _____.

incredible
  in—not

If it is unbelievable, we say it is _____.

A credulous person is one who believes things too
readily. ("It must be true. I read it in the paper!")
When something amazing happens, when you can hardly believe what you see or hear, an incredulous expression comes over your face. If a little green man
with horns suddenly materialized before you, no doubt
you would be overcome with a feeling of incredulity.

believable

To summarize: Something that is credible is _____

_____. Something incredible

not believable

is _____. A person who

credulous
  cred—believe
  ous—marked by

believes too easily is _____.

Something that you cannot at first believe, in spite

incredulous

of evidence, brings about an _____
look to your face; it creates in you a feeling of

incredulity

_____.

The testimony of two other reliable witnesses lent
credence to my story about sighting a flying saucer.

believability

What does credence mean here? _____

creditable

The actor gave a very _____
performance as Hamlet. ("able to be believed; de-
serving credit or praise)

Self-Test

1. Bill's account of the adventure was so _____ that none of us could take him seriously. (not believable)

2. Ten minutes after he received the check for one million dollars he still had an incredulous expression on his face. <u>Incredulous</u> means _____ _____.

3. Sherlock Holmes gave little <u>credence</u> to the theory that the Creeper was in reality a woman. Holmes thought the theory was: likely/unlikely/confirmed.

4. Vera did a very _____ job of writing up that report for the manager. (praiseworthy)

5. Teddy admitted readily that his actions were not in keeping with the Boy Scout creed. A <u>creed</u> is _____.

Answers to Self-Test

1. incredible 2. not believing 3. unlikely 4. creditable 5. a statement of belief

(13) CUR, COUR, run

Derivatives:

concurrently (kuhn KUR runt lee)
courier (KUR ee er)
current (KUR runt)
cursory (KURSS er ree)

excursion (eks KUR shun)
incursion (in KUR shun)
precursor (pre KUR sir)
recurrent (re KUR runt)

Prefixes	Suffixes
con—together	ier—one who
ex—outside	ent—marked by; that which
in—in, into	ion—act of
pre—before	ly—adverb ending
re—again, back	or—that which
	ory—marked by

current
cur—run
ent—that which

It is more difficult to swim against the _____ _____. ("that which runs"; running part of a stream; the swiftest part)

Marvin suffered from a recurrent illness. <u>Recurrent</u>

marked by
running back

literally means _____.
So a recurrent illness occurs again and again.

excursion

They planned a brief _____ into the countryside. (act of running outside)

The newspaper reported the latest incursions of ene-

acts of running into; invasions

my forces. What are <u>incursions</u>? _____

_____

Selma could not answer the question directed to her

cursory

because she had given the article only a _____ glance. (running)

A small power blackout in the East may be the pre-cursor of widespread power failures. A <u>precursor</u>

that which runs before

is what? _____

courier

A _____ arrived with a message from the king. (one who runs; runner)

concurrently
  con—together

Five different films are being shown _____ at the Festival Cinema Theatre. (an adverb meaning running together)

Self-Test

1. Since returning from a six months' vacation in the tropics, Mr. Small has been plagued by a _____ illness. (occurring again and again)

2. The ambassador laughed and admitted he was acting as little more than a diplomatic courier, bringing an important message from the President for the new premier. What is a <u>courier</u>? _____

3. The local farmers resented the summer tourists and thought of their pic-nics, hikes, and wood-gathering as the _____ of the enemy. (acts of running into; invasions)

4. The three cases of flu reported in Amador County may be the precursor of another epidemic. <u>Precursor</u> means _____.

5. The convention headquarters in the new Hilton hotel are large enough that three large groups can be accommodated concurrently. What does <u>con-currently</u> mean? _____

6. Amanda's Tours specializes in one-day _____ for senior citizens. (acts of running outside)

Answers to Self-Test

1. recurrent 2. a runner or messenger 3. incursions 4. that which runs before 5. running together 6. excursions

 14 DICT, say, speak, tell

Derivatives:

dictaphone (DIK tuh fone)   jurisdiction (jure iss DIK shun)
dictate (DIK tate)   predicate (PRED uh kate)
dictator (DIK tate er)   valedictorian (val uh dik TORE ee un)
edict (EE dikt)

Prefixes	Other roots	Suffixes
e—outside	phone—instrument for	ate—verb ending
pre—before	recording	ian—one who
	sound	or—one who
	juris—law	
	val—farewell	

he speaks it to her

When a boss <u>dictates</u> a letter to his stenographer, what does he do? _____

an instrument for recording the voice

If a stenographer is not available, a boss may dictate into a dictaphone. What is a <u>dictaphone</u>? _____

_____

one who speaks
  dict—speak
  or—one who

The <u>dictator</u> of a country is literally _____

_____. In actual usage, a <u>dictator</u> is a very powerful person who <u>tells</u> everyone else what to do.

valedictorian

<u>Vale</u> means "farewell." The person who delivers the farewell address for a graduating class is the _____

_____ (Traditionally, he is also the student with the highest grade average.)

The prince's early education was predicated on a study of Latin and Greek. Here <u>predicated</u> means that someone in authority (his parents or his tutors) spoke about the matter ahead of time and made a decision which was then followed. Thus, <u>predicated</u>

based on

means: based on/arranged so as to avoid.

<u>Juris</u> means "law." If something is outside the area in which a court can hear and decide ("speak on")

jurisdiction

cases, it is outside that court's _____.

speaks out
  e—out

An <u>edict</u> is something that _____
on a subject. Actually, an edict is a command or
order.

Self-Test

1. The judge said that such a matter was entirely outside the jurisdiction of

his court. <u>Jurisdiction</u> refers to _____

_____.

2. The revolutionary Atkins diet is predicated on the fact that carbohydrates
are largely responsible for allowing the body to store or use up fat. <u>Pred</u>-

<u>icated</u> means _____.

3. The controversy was finally resolved by a royal _____. (act
of speaking out; decision made by one in authority)

4. The opposition party feared that the new president was intent on becoming

a _____. (one ruling absolutely)

5. Nancie Jane is this year's valedictorian. What does the <u>valedictorian</u>

normally do at graduation? _____

6. Once a week the ranch foreman picks up the phone and _____
a long order of groceries to Sam Peckinpah. (speaks, says)

7. Miss Beardsley still has five letters to type from the _____.
(instrument for recording the voice)

Answers to Self-Test

1. the area in which a court can hear and decide on a case 2. based on; "spoken before" 3. edict 4. dictator 5. gives a farewell address 6. dictates
7. dictaphone

(15) DUCT, DUC, lead

Derivatives:
    aqueduct (AK wuh dukt)
    conduct (kun DUKT)
    deduce (dee DUCE)
    duct (DUKT)
    ductile (DUK tuhl)

    induction (in DUK shun)
    reduce (re DUCE)
    seduce (sih DUCE)
    seductive (sih DUK tiv)
    viaduct (VEYE uh dukt)

Prefixes	Other roots	Suffixes
con—together	aque—water	ile—marked by
de—down	via—road	ive—marked by
in—in		ion—act of, process
re—back, again		
se—away from		

conduct
  con—together
  duct—lead

John Masters will _____ the orchestra. (lead together)

The cost of black-and-white television sets has been reduced considerably. <u>Reduced</u> literally means

led back
  re—back
  duc—lead

_____.

In the narrowest sense <u>seduce</u> means "lead astray" sexually: John <u>seduced</u> Mary. In a broader sense it means simply to lead into wrongdoing. The adjective form <u>seductive</u>, on the other hand, describes something that allures or charms: <u>seductive</u> music, a <u>seductive</u> manner of speaking. To review, a friend

seduced

_____ you into disregarding your work and going to a movie. The movie was filled with

seductive

_____ brown-eyed maidens swaying to the rhythm of tropical drums.

bent
  duct—lead

<u>Ductile</u> metals like copper can be easily: bent/hardened. This is because their pliability allows for stretching and reshaping.

The channels that allow tears to flow from the eyes

ducts

are called tear _____. ("leaders")

The Romans gave us the <u>aqueduct</u>, which is a structure that

leads water
  aque—water
  duct—lead

ture that _____.

A structure used to lead a road (<u>via</u>) or train track across a valley, a gorge, or a part of a city is a

viaduct

_____.

The name given to the process whereby civilians are

induction

"led into" the armed services is called _____

_____.

If you <u>deduce</u> that someone is a Republican, your logic leads down from a generalization (Everyone here at the meeting is a Republican) to a specific case (John must be a Republican). Sherlock Holmes knew that a man who limps puts more weight on his good leg. In investigating a murder, Sherlock found footprints in the mud outside a library window. The impression of the left foot was much deeper. Sherlock therefore

deduced

_____ that the murderer was lame in the right leg. ("led down")

Self-Test

1. The _____ fragrance of tropical flowers greeted them even before they could see the island. (alluring; tending to lead astray)

2. Sherlock Holmes _____ that the thief must have been lefthanded. ("led down"; inferred from a general principle)

3. Two days after he reached the age of twenty-one the army notified him to report for induction. What is <u>induction</u>? _____

_____

4. Copper is a ductile metal. What does <u>ductile</u> mean? _____

5. What is the function of an air <u>duct</u>? _____

6. What would you call a structure that leads a road over a deep gorge?

_____

7. Some of the Roman _____ are still standing. (structures that carry water)

8. The warm, sunny weather seduced me into leaving the library and going outdoors. <u>Seduced</u> means _____

<u>Answers to Self-Test</u>

1. seductive 2. deduced 3. the process of being led into the armed forces
4. easily bent 5. to lead or bring air into a room 6. viaduct 7. aqueducts
8. led astray; persuaded into some form of wrongdoing

(16) FAC, FACT, FECT, FIC, FEAT, FEAS, FY, do, make

Derivatives:

efficient (ee FISH unt)
facile (FASS uhl)
facility (fuh SILL uh tee)
facsimile (fak SIM uh lee)
factory (FAK tree)
feasible (FEEZ uh buhl)

feat (FEET)
magnify (MAG nuh feye)
manufacture (man yoo FAK chure)
perfectionist (per FEK shun ist)
proficient (pro FISH unt)

<u>Prefixes</u>
ef—out
per—thoroughly
pro—forward

<u>Other roots</u>
magn—large
manu—hand

<u>Suffixes</u>
ile—able
ity—quality of
ient—marked by
ion—act of
ist—one who
ory—place

factory
  fact—made
  ory—place

A place where things are made is a _____ .

to make by hand
  manu—hand
  fact—made

If <u>manu</u> means "hand," what is the literal meaning of the verb <u>manufacture</u>? _____

ease

facility

A <u>facile</u> artist is "able to do"—that is, able to create things with: ease/difficulty. An ease at doing or making something is called a _____ .

a copy or
reproduction
  fac—make
  simil—similar

An American millionaire builds a home in New York that is a facsimile of a castle in Europe. If <u>simil</u> means "similar," what is a <u>facsimile</u>? _____

_____

perfectionist
  per—thoroughly
  fect—do
  ion—act of
  ist—one who

A person who has to do everything as thoroughly as possible is called a _____ .
(one who does thoroughly)

proficient
  pro—forward
  fic—do

If you can do something that requires advanced skill or knowledge, you are _____ .
(marked by making forward—that is, by making progress)

efficient
  ef—out

If you can do something without wasting time or energy, you are _____ .
("marked by making out"; able to bring about desired effects)

make larger
  magn—large
  fy—make

To <u>magnify</u> is to _____ .

classify

To group things into classes is to _____ .
("make classes")

done or made
  feas—do, make

If something is <u>feasible</u>, it can be _____ .

feats

Audiences generally applaud "things done" that show great strength or skill, such as acrobatic _____ .

Self-Test

1. Henry and his brother William were both <u>facile</u> writers. That is, they both wrote: poetically/strangely/easily.

2. The Murphys' summer home is a facsimile of Anne Hathway's cottage in England. What is a <u>facsimile</u>? _____

3. Stokes has a _____ for inspiring others to make a greater effort. (ease of doing something)

4. An _____ secretary would organize the office routine in such a way that everything got done on time with a minimum of effort. (able to bring about an effect without wasting time or energy)

5. Margaret told Harry that the TV comedy series THE ODD COUPLE is a story about a slob and a perfectionist who try to live together. A <u>perfectionist</u> is someone who _____.

6. Only a highly _____ craftsman like Mr. Donovan could command such a high fee for his work. (able to make progress; having advanced skill or knowledge)

7. Mr. Martin questioned whether or not it would be feasible to tear out the west wall of the delivery room. <u>Feasible</u> means _____
_____.

8. Righting that overturned car was certainly a _____ of strength! ("thing done")

<u>Answers to Self-Test</u>

1. easily 2. a copy or reproduction 3. facility 4. efficient 5. feels he must do everything as thoroughly as possible 6. proficient 7. able to be done 8. feat

(17) FER, LAT, bear, carry*

Derivatives:

conifer (KON uh fer)
coniferous (kuh NIF er us)
defer (dee FER)
deference (DEF er unce)
deferential (def er EN shuhl)
differentiate (dif fer EN she ate)
elation (ee LAY shun)

fertile (FERT uhl)
infer (in FER)
inference (IN fer unce)
proliferate (pro LIF er ate)
proliferation (pro liff er AY shun)
relate (ree LATE)

---

*FER and LAT are grouped together here because they have the same meaning.

Prefixes
de—down
dif—apart
in—in
pro—forward, forth

Other roots
proli—offspring

Suffixes
ate—verb ending
ation—process of
ion—act of
ence—quality of
ile—marked by
ial—marked by
ous—marked by

bear
  fer—bear
  ile—marked by

If an animal is <u>fertile</u>, it is able to _____ offspring. In order to "bear" them, it must "carry" them in embryo form; hence, the similarity of the two meanings.

conifer
  con—cone
  fer—bear

A pine tree, which "bears cones," is a _____

_____ .

coniferous

The Norway pine is a _____ tree. (marked by bearing cones)

proliferation

If <u>proli</u> means "offspring," the process of reproducing new parts, offshoots or cells is called _____

_____ .

you keep getting
more new things
to do

If you say your work is <u>proliferating</u>, what do you mean? _____

carry down
  de—down
  fer—carry

Two of you must make a decision. You decide to defer to your friend. Literally, <u>defer</u> means _____

_____ . Temporarily you "carry down" your importance to a lower level than his. The voluntary respect you show older people, bosses, and

deference

the like is called _____ . Most

deferential

of us like it when others treat us in a _____ manner. (marked by deference)

carried apart
  dif—apart
  fer—carry

Two things that are <u>different</u> are literally _____

_____ . To make a distinction between two things—that is, to carry them apart—is to

differentiate

_____ them.

Two competitive women meet on Easter Sunday, each eyeing the outfit the other is wearing. Helen says to Margaret, "Oh, my dear, what a lovely dress! I've always liked it since you first wore it ten years ago."

Helen implies that Margaret is not stylish or cannot afford anything new. If Margaret gets this meaning, she is said to <u>infer</u> it. The one who puts in a hidden message <u>implies</u>; the one who uncovers the hidden

infers

message _____. Helen's statement contains a negative <u>implication</u>; if Margaret makes

inference

the correct _____, she will be offended.

An explorer returns from some exciting adventures in the Arctic. His friends are eager to hear him

relate

_____ his experiences. ("carry back"; give an account of)

It seemed as though all her dreams had come true,

elation

and Thelma felt a sense of _____. ("act of being carried outside" oneself; state of joy or pride)

Self-Test

1. Miss James approached the supervisor carefully in a _____ manner. (showing respect)

2. If my inference is correct, you imply that I am lazy and irresponsible.

    What is an <u>inference</u>? _____

3. In despair he said, "The problems facing this company keep <u>proliferating</u>!" He means that: new problems keep popping up/the problems are getting more difficult/the problems cost more to solve

4. If you have a conscience, you cannot help _____ing between good and bad in your own behavior. (making a distinction)

5. Mr. Dunn planted only conifers because they take less watering. What are <u>conifers</u>? _____

6. The turtle is said to be very _____. (able to bear offspring)

7. When he was announced the winner of the contest, Hamilton expressed his

    _____ by shouting "Hey, hey!" and waving to the audience.

Answers to Self-Test

1. deferential 2. a process of uncovering a hidden message 3. new problems keep popping up 4. differentiating 5. cone-bearing trees 6. fertile 7. elation

(18)   FID, faith

Derivatives:

affidavit (af fuh DAY vit)
bona fide (BON uh FIDE)
confidant (kon fuh DAHNT)
confide (kun FIDE)
diffident (DIF uh dunt)

fidelity (fuh DELL uh tee)
infidelity (in fuh DELL uh tee)
infidel (IN fuh dell)
perfidious (per FID ee us)

Prefixes	Suffixes
af—to, toward	ant—one who
con—together, with	el—one who
dif—apart	ent—marked by
e—outside, out of	ion—act of
in—not	ity—act of
per—thoroughly	ous—marked by

faith

When you <u>confide</u> in someone, you show that you have complete _____ in him. The person in

confidant
  con—with
  fid—faith

whom you most often confide is your _____

_____. (one you have faith with)

faith

<u>Bona</u> means "good." A <u>bona fide</u> offer to buy a house is made "in good _____.''

The marriage vows require a couple to pledge their <u>fidelity</u> to each other. What does fidelity mean?

faithfulness
(especially sexual)

_____

infidelity

If one of them later breaks that pledge, he is guilty of _____.

affidavit
  af—toward
  fid—faith

A statement written down and sworn to be true is an

_____. ("that which is faithful toward")

diffident

A person who is "apart from faith" in himself is very shy or _____.

infidel

During the Crusades the Christians fought the _____

_____. (those not of the faith, here the Christian faith)

faith

A <u>perfidious</u> action breaks _____ with someone: The legal maneuvers of Ted's partner

perfidious

were _____ because they brought about Ted's financial ruin. (marked by thoroughly breaking faith)

Self-Test

1. Mr. Parks insisted that he had received a bona fide invitation to join the law firm of Miller, Sarks, and Warnes. <u>Bona fide</u> means _____ _____ .

2. In spite of their personality differences, General Patton and General Bradley treated each other as _____ . (a person regularly confided in)

3. Mrs. Wiggs felt it wise to overlook her husband's occasional _____ _____ . (sexual unfaithfulness)

4. Mr. Thornton himself could not appear at the trial, but he left an affidavit. What is an <u>affidavit</u>? _____

5. Jack had a reputation for being unfriendly whereas in reality he was simply diffident. <u>Diffident</u> means _____ .

6. Mr. Horn's action in revealing our plans to the opposition party is _____ _____ . (marked by a complete lack of faith)

7. We always offered so many excuses for not attending Sunday school that Aunt Polly branded us her little _____ . (those who are not of the faith)

Answers to Self-Test

1. in good faith 2. confidants 3. infidelity 4. a written statement sworn to be a faithful account 5. shy; lacking faith 6. perfidious 7. infidels

(19) FUS, FUND, FOUND, pour

Derivatives:

confuse (kun FUSE)
effusive (ih FEW siv)
foundry (FOUN dree)
infuse (in FUSE)

profusion (pro FEW zhun)
refund (REE fund)
refuse (re FUSE)
suffuse (suh FUSE)

Prefixes
con—with, together
ef—out
in—in
pro—forth, forward
re—back
suf—under

Suffixes
ive—marked by
ry—place where
ion—condition of

He offered his help, but she refused it. Refuse is such a common word it is difficult to think of a synonym for it. But its original, literal meaning is

"pour back"
re—back
fus—pour

vivid: refuse means "_____."

Confuse also has a vivid literal meaning: confuse

"pour together"
con—together
fus—pour

means "_____." Think of that meaning as you read this sentence: He knew that he was aging because his memories often became confused.

He infused his own enthusiasm into his fellow workers. What does infused mean here? "_____

"poured into";
that is, he
inspired his fellow
workers

_____"

profusion

The garden was a _____ of flowers in all colors. (act of pouring forth)

suffused

Just at sunset the clouds were _____ with pink. (poured under; underspread)

refund

In two days you will receive a _____ from the national office. (that which is poured back; money given back)

The workers are going on strike at the iron foundry.

a place where iron
is melted and poured
into casts

What do you think an iron foundry is? _____

_____

Three days after our disagreement, her greeting was as effusive as ever. Think of the literal meaning of effusive and then describe the kind of greeting she

showing much
feeling; gushy
ef—out
fus—pour
ive—marked by

gave. _____

Self-Test

1. The meadow was covered with a _____ of wildflowers. (act of pouring forth)

2. The sergeant tried to infuse his men with his own sense of responsibility.

Infuse means to _____.

3.　Their appreciation was so effusive it almost embarrassed him.　What
does <u>effusive</u> mean? _____

4.　The flowers were pale cream lightly _____ with pink.
(underspread)

5.　The statues were sent back to the _____, where they
would be melted down and recast.　(place where metals are melted and
poured into casts)

6.　If the tribal chieftain offers you some beer, you must not _____
it.　("pour back"; turn it down)

Answers to Self-Test

1. profusion　2. "pour into"; inspire　3. showing more feeling than is warrant-
ed; gushy; "pouring out"　4. suffused　5. foundry　6. refuse

(20)　GRAD, GRESS, step, go

Derivatives:
<blockquote>
aggressive (uh GRESS iv)　　　egress (EE gress)
degrade (dee GRADE)　　　　　progressive (pro GRESS iv)
digress (deye GRESS)　　　　　retrogression (RET row gress shun)
</blockquote>

Prefixes	Suffixes
ag—to, toward	ive—marked by
de—down	ion—act of
di—apart	
e—out, out of	
pro—forward	
retro—backward	

degrade
　de—down
　grad—step

If a person's actions make him "step down" to a lower
level of behavior or existence, they _____
him.

progressive
　pro—forward
　gress—go

An illness that keeps "going forward" and becoming
worse is a _____ illness.
<u>Progressive</u> may also have a positive meaning, as
when a mayor is complimented by being called progressive (going forward; wanting improvement in
government).

setback or
deterioration
　retro—backward
　gress—go

An ill person who suffers a general <u>retrogression</u> is
undergoing a:　slow improvement/setback or deterioration.

aggressive
 ag—toward
 gress—step

A person who is quick to assert himself, to "step toward" others, is an _____ person.

A lecturer is discussing the reasons why the South seceded from the Union. Then he digresses and for a few minutes discusses the problems of commuting to and from a large urban center. What does digress

to turn aside
from the main
subject
 di—apart
 gress—go

mean? _____

exits
 e—out
 gress

If egress from a building is insufficient to satisfy the fire inspector, there are not enough: exits/doormen.

Self-Test

1. The marble statues and columns in Venice are subject to _____ deterioration and decay. ("marked by going forward"; advancing)

2. The egress of people from the Hollywood Bowl began at ten o'clock and lasted nearly two hours. Egress means _____.

3. The retrogression of a man's faculties would mean their: worsening/ gradual improvement.

4. Lou Ann was surprised to discover that she, too, had some _____ tendencies. (determined pursuit of one's ends; self-assertive)

5. The brainwashing techniques were intended to break down a prisoner's resistance, to _____ him in his own eyes. (to lower in moral or intellectual character; "step down")

6. When her husband seemed on the verge of digressing, Mildred would cough politely. Digressing means _____

_____.

Answers to Self-Test

1. progressive 2. movement to the outside; going out 3. worsening 4. aggressive 5. degrade 6. leaving the main subject in a discussion; "going apart"

JAC, JECT, throw, hurl

Derivatives:

abject (ab JEKT)
adjective (AJ ik tiv)
conjecture (kun JEK shure)
dejected (dee JEK tuhd)
ejaculation (ee JAK yoo LAY shun)
eject (ee JEKT)
injection (in JEK shun)

interject (in ter JEKT)
objective (ub JEK tiv)
project (pro JEKT)
projectile (pro JEK tuhl)
reject (ree JEKT)
subjection (sub JEK shun)

Prefixes
ab—down
ad—to, toward
con—together
de—down
e—out
in—in, into
inter—between
ob—against
pro—forward
re—back
sub—under

Suffixes
ive—that which
ion—act of
ile—that which

ejaculation
  e—out
  jac—throw

A sudden, brief, often very emotional "throwing out" of words is an _____. A discharge of semen is also called an <u>ejaculation</u>.

hurl forward
  pro—forward
  ject—throw

If you had a time machine, you could project yourself into the future. Literally, <u>project</u> means _____

_____.

projectile

An explosive "hurled forward" from a gun, cannon, or bazooka is a _____.

act of throwing
into

A nurse administered the injection. <u>Injection</u> means

_____. In this case, medicine is injected into a patient's body, but a large grant of money to a bankrupt company might also be called an

injection

_____.

objective
  ob—against

What is your educational _____?
(thing thrown against; thing aimed at)

Even though she was down to her last dime, she rejected the offer of a small loan. <u>Rejected</u> means

thrown back;
refused
  re—back

_____.

adjective

An _____ modifies a noun, as in
"a tall tree." (that which is thrown toward)

subjection

The _____ of the mountain tribes
took five years. (act of throwing under; bringing
under the control of someone else)

It is a matter of conjecture whether or not Stanley
will return. What do you think conjecture means?

a guess; literally,
"that which is
thrown together"

_____

ejects

At the mere touch of a button the machine _____
stamps. (throws out)

Dejected and abject both have the literal meaning
"thrown down," but whereas dejected means "low-
ered in spirits," abject means "miserable or wretched." After they lost the game, the team members

dejected

were _____. The worst kind of

abject

poverty is called _____ poverty.

Wilson tapped Mrs. Bowes on the shoulder and said,

interject

"May I please _____ a word or
two?" ("throw between")

Self-Test

1. Lawrence had packed some snow tightly into a small ball, and he aimed

   the _____ directly at Mr. Crowe's hat. (object
   hurled forward)

2. The pilot survived because he was ejected moments before the crash.

   Ejected means the pilot was _____.

3. The first rejection slip made him feel _____. (low in
   spirits)

4. The prisoners of war reported they lived under _____
   conditions. (miserable or wretched)

5. Diana dismissed his explanation of the delay in taking off from the airport

   as mere conjecture. What is a conjecture? _____

   _____

6. Women no longer appear to desire living in _____ to their men. (condition of being under the influence or control of someone else)

7. Each cadet had first to determine his military objective. What is an <u>ob-jective</u>? _____

8. The fever can be controlled by an _____ of antibiotic. ("act of throwing into")

9. The news of the tragedy had a strange effect on her. She sat down on the ground and cried, "Here be a poor orphan! Here be a sufferin' old wom-an!" These and similar _____ continued for a full five minutes. (short, sudden emotional utterances)

10. Douglas and Sandy were almost at blows; it was certainly time to try to interject a note of warning. <u>Interject</u> means to _____.

11. The speaker was _____ a bright future in which all social and economic problems had been settled. ("throwing forward")

Answers to Self-Test

1. projectile 2. thrown out 3. dejected 4. abject 5. a guess; something "thrown together" 6. subjection 7. goal aimed at; something to be "thrown against" 8. injection 9. ejaculations 10. "throw between" 11. projecting

(22)   MAL, bad

Derivatives:

maladroit (MAL uh droit)   malfeasance (mal FEEZ unce)
malady (MAL uh dee)   malefactor (MAL uh fak ter)
malaria (muh LARE ee uh)   malignant (muh LIG nunt)
malediction (mal uh DIK shun)   malnutrition (mal new TRISH un)
malevolent (muh LEV uh lunt)   malodorous (mal ODE er us)

Other roots	Suffixes
ig—do, drive, carry on	ance—act of
	ant—marked by
vol—will, attitude	ion—act of
dict—say, speak	ous—marked by
feas, fact—do	or—one who

A tumor that is no longer growing or spreading is benign (of good origin); a harmful, often cancerous

malignant
  mal—bad
  ig—do

tumor is _____. (marked by doing bad)

Because I had not crossed her palm with enough sil-

curses; "bad speech"
mal—bad
dict—speak

ver, the fortune teller hurled maledictions at me as I left the tent. What are <u>maledictions</u>? _____

_____

marked by bad will; having an evil intention
mal—bad
vol—will

The bully grabbed Tom's arm, and there was a mal-evolent look in his eye. <u>Malevolent</u> means _____

_____

some kind of wrongdoing
feas—do

What would be meant by <u>malfeasance</u> in public office?

_____

maladroit

<u>Adroit</u> people are very graceful, especially in using their bodies. What would people be called who are very clumsy? _____

malodorous

As a protective mechanism skunks throw off a

_____ scent. (marked by a bad odor)

malnutrition

An improper diet can lead to _____. (bad nutrition)

bad

<u>Malaria</u> was once thought to be caused by _____ air.

one who does something bad
mal—bad
factor—one who does

What is a <u>malefactor</u>? _____

_____

bad

No one could decide what was the cause of the <u>malady</u> that overtook the princess. A <u>malady</u> is literally "something _____ "—an illness or a disease.

Self-Test

1. In two days the dead fish were _____, to say the least. (bad-smelling)

2. Shakespeare portrays Shylock as a malevolent old man who wants revenge in the form of a pound of human flesh. <u>Malevolent</u> means _____

_____.

3. For years he has been suffering from a mysterious _____. (sickness, disease)

4. In a very critical editorial Mr. March referred to the action of the Board of Supervisors as malfeasance in public office. <u>Malfeasance</u> is _____

_____ .

5. Miss Taylor is too maladroit to be a good waitress. <u>Maladroit</u> means: clumsy/money-hungry/young.

6. As she hurried down the stairs, she could hear the old drunk's _____

_____ ringing in her ears. (curses)

7. The presence of a _____ tumor in her left breast meant that she had to undergo a mastectomy. (doing evil; continuing to grow and spread)

8. People may be eating large quantities of food—improper food, that is— and yet show signs of _____ . (bad nutrition)

9. Eventually the old colonel became so twisted in mind that he thought any-one who opposed him in any way whatsoever was a malefactor. What is

a <u>malefactor</u>? _____

Answers to Self-Test

1. malodorous 2. marked by bad will or evil intentions 3. malady 4. wrong-doing 5. clumsy 6. maledictions 7. malignant 8. malnutrition 9. someone who does evil things

(23) MIT, MISS, send

Derivatives:
admit (ad MIT)
commission (kum MISH un)
emissary (EM uh sare ee)
emission (ee MISH un)
intermission (in ter MISH un)
missile (MISS uhl)

missive (MISS iv)
premise (PREM iss)
promise (PROM iss)
remission (ree MISH un)
remittance (ree MIT unce)
submissive (sub MISS iv)
transmit (trans MIT)

Prefixes
ad—to, toward
com—with, together
e—out of
inter—between
pre—before
pro—forward
re—back
sub—under
trans—across

Suffixes
ance—that which
ary—one who
ile—that which
ion—act of
ive—that which

Choose the derivatives that fit the literal meanings listed below:

remittance
  re—back
  mit—send

(Money) sent back: _____

transmit

To send across, as a message: _____

promise

A guarantee "sent forth": _____

A period of time "sent between," as at a play or con-

intermission

cert: _____

admit

To send toward (allow): _____

A person sent outside his own country to accomplish

emissary
  e—outside
  mis—out

good will can be called an _____
of good will.

A police commission is literally a group of people

"sent together"

"_____" to accomplish some
task.

A statement or generalization "sent before" and as-

premise

sumed to be true is a _____. Here
are examples of premises used in a syllogism, a type
of reasoning chain you studied earlier:
    Major premise: Misbehaving children should be
           scolded.
    Minor premise: Dennis is a misbehaving child.
    Conclusion: Dennis should be scolded.

The suffix -ile means "that which." Nowadays a

missile

self-propelled bomb or rocket is called a _____

_____. (that which is sent through the air)

Although the use is no longer current, a letter can

sent

be called a missive—"something _____."

Miss can sometimes have the meaning "let go." What
do we mean if we say that a wife is submissive?

she yields
("lets go under")
to the authority
or control of her
husband

_____

_____

For reasons that were not clear to his doctors, Howard enjoyed a remission of the arthritic pain that
plagued him. What does remission mean in this con-

The pain left him
temporarily

text? _____

sending out
pollutants

An efficent smog-control device will cut down the
emission of pollutants from gasoline motors. What
does emission mean in this context? _____
_____

Self-Test

1. Jazz musicians have often been the most successful emissaries of good
    will in Europe and Russia. What are emissaries? _____
    _____

2. I agree with your major _____ but not your conclusion
    that draft evaders should be imprisoned. (a generalization assumed to be
    true)

3. A comprehensive system of baffles greatly cut down the _____
    of noise. (sending out)

4. The examining team at the hospital said not to expect any remission of
    Clara's illness. Remission means _____.

5. Please enclose your _____ of $14.95 in the
    envelope provided and send at once. (payment)

6. _____ children are not necessarily the "best"
    children; they may be repressed emotionally. (yielding to the authority
    or control of someone else)

7. Two members of the city art_____ will judge the
    sidewalk art display next Sunday afternoon. (group "sent together" to
    handle a particular task)

8. A clergyman sends out a missive to the members of his congregation.
    What would we call a missive today? _____

9. What do we call something "sent" through the air, such as a rocket or
    bomb? _____

10. The sign said, "Smoking only during _____." (time
    between acts of a play, etc.)

Answers to Self-Test

1. those sent out of the country 2. premise 3. emission 4. temporary going
away 5. remittance 6. submissive 7. commission 8. a letter 9. a missile
10. intermission

PENS, PEND, POND, hang, weigh

Derivatives:

appendage (uh PEN dij)   expend (eks PEND)
appendix (uh PEN diks)   impend (im PEND)
compensation (kom pen SAY shun) pendant (PEN dunt)
dependent (dee PEN dunt)   pensive (PEN siv)
dispensary (dis PEN sir ee)   ponderous (PON der us)
dispense (dis PENCE)   recompense (REK um penss)

Prefixes
ap—on
com—with, together
de—down, from
ex—out
im—over
re—again, back

Suffixes
ant—that which
ant—one who
ary—place of
ous—marked by

The words derived from this root were associated originally with the process of weighing out money or some form of currency on scales (the old-fashioned kind, with two pans opposite each other hanging from a point of balance, as the "scales of justice" are us-

"weigh out"
  ex—out
  pend—weigh

ually pictured). Thus, to expend money is to "_____

_____" money—that is, spend it.

If you give someone compensation for the work he has

"weigh together"
  com—together
  pens—weigh

done for you, you "_____"
the work and the money owed him, so the work and money will balance each other in the scale.

payment

Compensation is thus: a gift/payment.

If you do something for someone else without thought of recompense, you do it without expecting to be:

paid back

appreciated/paid back.

something that
hangs from a
chain or wire

What kind of ornament is a pendant? _____

_____

Visualize a baby or small child in its mother's arms and you will see why it is called a dependent. A de-

"one that hangs
from"; one who
relies on another
for support.

pendent is _____

_____.

Occasionally the prefix ap- means "on." An appendix

"that which hangs on"; an addition

something hanging on to the body

awaiting action

a storm that is about to occur
  im—over
  pend—hang

dispensary

pond

ponderous

weighing a decision

weighing

heavy

at the end of a book is what? _____

An arm or leg is technically an appendage. What visual image does <u>appendage</u> bring to mind? _____

A new environmental control act is <u>pending</u> in Congress. It is: awaiting action/causing controversy.

What is an <u>impending</u> storm? _____

_____

People who <u>dispense</u> (give out) medicines or medical advice for free or for a small charge work in a place (-<u>ary</u>) called a _____ .

Most of the machinery used in heavy construction work is ponderous equipment. What word part indicates that <u>ponderous</u> equipment weighs so much that it is slow and awkward to handle? _____
A book or discussion that is dull and tiresome is also _____ . (weighty)

If you are <u>pondering</u> what to do next, you are doing what? _____

Bill is in a <u>pensive</u> mood. He is _____ ing some sad or sober ideas.

In a long-running TV series the Cartwright family owned a big ranch in Nevada called the <u>Ponderosa</u>. The ranch got its name from the many <u>ponderosa</u> pine trees that grew there. <u>Ponderosa</u> pines are literally " _____ pines."

Self-Test

1. The smile on your face is _____ for all my labors. (payment—two words will fit here)

2. The elephants began their _____ trek across the Serengeti. (heavy; slow and unwieldy)

3. She is in a pensive frame of mind. <u>Pensive</u> means _____

_____ .

4. You may pick up your medicine in the hospital dispensary. A <u>dispensary</u> is _____ .

5.   What she called a _____ was no more than an uneven
     piece of rock suspended from a leather thong. (hanging ornament)

6.   The Coast Guard warned small boats of impending danger. <u>Impending</u>
     means _____.

7.   A bill authorizing the state to purchase more land for recreation is still
     pending. What does <u>pending</u> mean? _____

8.   A person's limbs can be thought of as _____ to his
     body. (parts hanging on to the body)

9.   The supplemental material usually attached to the end of a piece of writ-
     ing, such as a book, is called an _____.

Answers to Self-Test

1. recompense or compensation 2. ponderous 3. weighing sad or sober
thoughts; reflective 4. a place where medicine or medical advice is given
out for free or for a small charge 5. pendant 6. about to happen; "hanging
over" 7. awaiting action; hanging 8. appendages 9. appendix

(25)   PLIC, PLI, PLY, fold, bend

Derivatives:
    compliance (kum PLEYE unce)   implicit (im PLISS it)
    complicate (KOM pluh kate)   multiplicity (mull tuh PLISS uh tee)
    complication (kom pluh KAY shun)   pliant (PLEYE unt)
    complicity (kum PLISS uh tee)   replica (REP luh kuh)
    duplicity (due PLISS uh tee)   triplicate (TRIP luh cut)
    explicit (eks PLISS it)

Prefixes	Other roots	Suffixes
com—with, together	du—two	ance—act of
ex—out of	multi—many	ant—relating to
im—in, within	tri—three	ate—verb ending
re—again		ation—act of, state of
		it—marked by
		ity—act of, state of

folds
  tri—three
  plic—fold

A letter typed in <u>triplicate</u> makes three _____.
or copies but the word is commonly used to mean
the original plus two copies.

a copy or
reproduction

<u>Replica</u> means "that which is folded again." A <u>repli-</u>
<u>ca</u> of a famous building in Europe would be: a copy
or reproduction/something without similarities to
anything else.

If you "fold your life together," you mix it up or

complicate
  com—together
  plic—fold

_____ it. Almost nobody gets by without a little complication in his life. What does <u>complication</u> mean in this context? _____

a confused state
of affairs

_____

"many folds"
  multi—many
  ply—fold

<u>Multiply</u> literally means "_____." To <u>multiply</u> your chances for success means to make many "folds" or increases. A retired man says, "There is such a <u>multiplicity</u> of things to enjoy, I can't imagine ever becoming bored." What does he

There is such a
great variety of
things to enjoy.

mean? _____

_____

A friend accuses Tom of <u>duplicity</u>. If <u>du</u> means

double-dealing or
deceitfulness

"double," what is Tom accused of? _____

_____

"folded together"

<u>Complicity</u> literally means "_____

_____." If a person is charged

a partner in crime

with <u>complicity</u> in a crime, he is: a partner in crime/ an innocent bystander.

He is readily
influenced ("bent")
by others.

How would you characterize a <u>pliant</u> person? _____

_____

yield to

A sergeant has the <u>compliance</u> of his men in performing a task. They: (resist/yield to) him.

explicit

The boss's orders are _____; they are clearly stated. ("folded out"; unfolded)

If someone's opinion of you is not clearly stated but

implicit

implied ("folded in"), that opinion is _____

_____.

Self-Test

1. The attorney general charged him with complicity in the murder of the union leader. <u>Complicity</u> means _____

_____.

2. They got lost because Harry's instructions were not _____ enough. (clearly stated; "folded out")

3. To persuade his wife to move to California with him, Mr. Noble promised
    to build her a _____ of the home she loved in New
    York. (copy; something "folded again")

4. Modern literature represents many different viewpoints and offers an
    amazing variety of choices, so much so that critics often refer to this as
    the age of _____ . (a great number of choices;
    "many folds")

5. We forwarded the letter to Mr. Furness in <u>compliance</u> with your request.
    That is, the letter was forwarded: in addition to your request/as you re-
    quested/contrary to your request.

6. Lady Margaret rebuked him sharply. "Your guilt is implicit in your man-
    ner of speaking about the young lady." <u>Implicit</u> means _____
    _____ .

7. At that age most children are quite _____ . (easily
    molded; readily influenced)

8. The report should be typed in _____ . (an original
    and two copies; "three folds")

9. Ronald was heartbroken by what he imagined to be his older brother's du-
    plicity. What does <u>duplicity</u> mean? _____

Answers to Self-Test

1. involvement; being "folded together" 2. explicit 3. replica 4. multiplicity
5. as you requested 6. not clearly stated but implied; "folded in" 7. pliant
8. triplicate 9. double-dealing; deceitfulness

(26)   SED, SID, SESS, sit

Derivatives:
    assiduous (uh SID jew us)   sedentary (SED un tare ee)
    reside (ree ZIDE)   sediment (SED uh munt)
    residual (ree ZID jew uhl)   subsidiary (sub SID ee air ee)
    sedate (suh DATE)   subsidy (SUB suh dee)
    sedative (SED uh tiv)   supersede (soo per SEED)

Prefixes	Suffixes
as—to, toward	al—marked by
re—back	ary—marked by
sub—under	ary—that which
super—above, beyond	ate—marked by
	ive—that which
	ment—that which
	ous—marked by

sitting

Sedentary occupations involve a great deal of _____

_____ .

replace

Jet planes have <u>superseded</u> propeller planes. Literally jet planes "sit above" propeller planes now in importance. A synonym for <u>supersede</u> would be: replace/parallel.

calm

Queen Victoria was often described as a <u>sedate</u> woman. She did sit at court a great deal, no doubt, but the adjective means that she was: calm and dignified/ excitable. To settle someone's nerves or calm him

sedative

down a doctor often prescribes a _____ .
(<u>-ive</u> = that which)

As a beaker of muddy water clears, <u>sediment</u> is formed in the bottom of the glass. What is <u>sediment</u>?

the substance that
settles to the
bottom

_____

sit back
  re—back
  sid—sit

The place where you <u>reside</u> is the place where you

" _____ " and take your comfort.

residual

A <u>residue</u> is something left over, something that settles back. Things made from leftovers are _____

_____ products. (of or pertaining to residue)

How would you characterize an <u>assiduous</u> worker?

He "sits toward"
his work busily and
attentively.
  as—toward
  sid—sit

_____

_____

having a meeting,
sitting

If Congress or some similar group is in <u>session</u>, what is it doing? _____

subside

When storms, strong emotions, or fast-paced activities lessen in intensity, they are said to _____

_____ . ("sit under")

assists or
supplements

A large company has the controlling interest in two smaller companies which it designates as its <u>subsidiaries</u>. A <u>subsidiary</u>: (assists or supplements/competes against) the main company.

Literally a <u>subsidy</u> was once "reserve troops," initially coming from the idea of extra soldiers who sat near the action at hand. Today when a government gives money or assistance to a private person or company whose enterprise will benefit the public, it

subsidy is called a _____.

Self-Test

1. Eleanor sat opposite the judge and his wife, looking queenly and _____ _____. (calm and dignified)

2. Senator Brooks asked for additional farm subsidies. What is a <u>subsidy</u>?

   _____

3. Mr. Fullerton commended Paul for the <u>assiduous</u> way in which he kept the accounts up to date. Fullerton was: praising Paul's work/telling Paul the accounts were badly handled/laughing at Paul for bothering with accounts.

4. The health lecturer warned that leading too _____ a life could seriously damage the heart. (marked by sitting)

5. They could not leave the cave until the storm subsided. <u>Subsided</u> means

   _____

6. After the flood the ground floor of the house was covered with a four-inch layer of _____. (two words will fit here)

7. Mildred was still unable to calm down after taking a _____. (drug used to settle nerves)

8. The star of a TV series often signs a contract that allows him residual payments if the series is used as a rerun. What does <u>residual</u> mean?

   _____

9. A company that operates independently but is under the control of another company is called a _____.

Answers to Self-Test

1. sedate 2. assistance given to a person or company whose enterprise should benefit the public 3. praising Paul's work 4. sedentary 5. lessened in intensity; "settled under" 6. sediment or residue 7. sedative 8. leftover or additional; "marked by settling back" 9. subsidiary

27 SCRIB, SCRIPT, write

Derivatives:

ascribe (uh SKRIBE)	nondescript (NON duh SKRIPT)
circumscribe (sir kum SKRIBE)	proscribe (pro SKRIBE)
conscription (kun SKRIP shun)	scribble (SKRIB uhl)
describe (duh SKRIBE)	subscribe (sub SKRIBE)

Prefixes
as—to, toward
circum—around
con—down
de—down
non—not
pro—forward
sub—under

Suffixes
ion—act of

scribble

If you write a note quickly and carelessly, your handwriting may look like _____.

"write down"
de—down
scrib—write

To describe yourself, you would "_____ _____" your most distinctive features— those things that make you different from others.

is not

A nondescript person (is/is not) very different or unique.

under

Martha subscribes to Playgirl Magazine. She "_____ _____ writes" it or supports it with her money. Explain what subscribe means in this sentence:

She supports
the idea

Martha subscribes to socialized medicine. _____

limited

Our vacation this year will be circumscribed by a lack of money. It will be "written around" by money and will thus be: limited/avoided. Mrs. Mooney

circumscribe

tried to restrict or _____ her daughter's social activities. ("write around")

assigned

Several reputable critics have ascribed the painting to Leonardo da Vinci. That means they have: assigned/withdrawn da Vinci's name. Your answer is

write toward
a—toward
scrib—write

proved by the literal meaning of ascribe: to _____ _____.

Medicines are prescribed by doctors. Certain dangerous or unlawful acts are proscribed (forbidden) by those in authority. The antibiotic was

prescribed

_____ by Doctor Bailey. Black-

proscribed

market trading was _____ by the
Commanding Officer.

Occasionally the prefix <u>con-</u> means "down." What
is the term identifying the process whereby the law
compels young men of military age to be enrolled

conscription

("written down") in the military service? _____

Self-Test

1. Safety officers _____ the decrease in highway
    fatalities to the lowered speed limits. (assign; "write toward")

2. Illness and personal problems greatly <u>circumscribed</u> his output of essays.
    That is, his output was _____.

3. Many people feel that smoking in public buildings and public transportation
    services should be proscribed. <u>Proscribed</u> means: forbidden/encouraged/
    surveyed.

4. Eunice has always _____ to the idea that hard work
    and responsibility make life interesting and worthwhile. (supported; un-
    derwritten)

5. The General has always believed in the voluntary _____
    of men for the armed forces. (enrollment)

6. Despite his superior intelligence and forceful personality, John has con-
    vinced himself that he is a completely nondescript person. What does

    <u>nondescript</u> mean? _____

Answers to Self-Test

1. ascribe 2. limited; restricted; "written around" 3. forbidden 4. sub-
scribed 5. conscription 6. not different or unique

(28)   SENT, SENS, feel

Derivatives:

dissension (dih SEN shun)
dissent (dih SENT)
presentiment (pre ZENT uh munt)
sensory (SENSE er ee)
sensual (SENSE yoo uhl)

sentiment (SENT uh munt)
sentimentality (sent uh men TAL
  uh tee)
sensuous (SEN shoo us)

Prefixes
dis—apart
pre—before

Suffixes
al—characterized by
ion—act of, state of
ity—state of
ment—state of
ory—characterized by
ous—characterized by

An impression that affects your ability to see, hear,

sensory

taste, touch, and smell is a _____ impression. Sensual and sensuous are adjectives that pertain to the bodily senses but are used in different ways. Sensuous most commonly means enjoying the pleasures of the senses: a sensuous love of colors and textures, the sensuous comfort of a warm bed on a cold night. Sensual, on the other hand, commonly implies a criticism—caring too much for the pleasures of the body, putting them ahead of the mind or soul: a man of a low, sensual nature; a book filled with sensual overtones. Distinguish these words in the following sentences. The prophet warned him to

sensual

put aside such _____ desires. She

sensuous

delighted in the _____ thrill of running her hands over the expensive furs.

feeling beforehand

A presentiment of danger is a: (feeling beforehand/ unrecognized feeling) that something bad is about to happen.

Sentiment is a feeling, especially of a tender or refined kind: the sentiment expressed by a mother for her baby. Sentimentality, on the other hand, is a gushy, over-emotional expression of feeling that does not seem quite justified: the sentimentality of a drunk who cries and keeps telling everyone how much he loves his wife. When people are sentimental, they usually exaggerate their feelings—and enjoy doing so. (Who hasn't taken a sentimental journey down mem-

ory lane?) So a justifiable tender feeling is _____

sentiment

_____, while an exaggerated, gushy,

sentimentality

over-emotional feeling is _____.

Mr. Backus proposed building a scenic highway through the center of the grape country. Immediately there was dissension in the group. Dissension

quarreling
  dis—apart
  sens—feeling

means: agreement/quarreling.

Whereas <u>dissension</u> means a hard feeling caused by differences of opinion, the word <u>dissent</u> is the actual difference of opinion or the right to feel differently: Political <u>dissent</u> is a part of the American system. To review: quarreling and the bad feeling brought

dissension   on by differences of opinion is called _____

_____; a difference of opinion is called

dissent   _____.

Self-Test

1.   Feeling the warm sun tanning the skin is one of the _____ pleasures of summer vacation. (marked by enjoying the pleasures of the senses)

2.   The instructor blindfolded me, placed me in a seat suspended from a chain. and asked me to describe my _____ impressions as he moved me in various directions at various speeds. (relating to the ability to see, hear, touch, taste, and smell)

3.   The prosecuting attorney denounced her as being a selfish, corrupt, sensual woman. <u>Sensual</u> means _____

_____.

4.   Polly resigned as president of the women's bridge club, saying she felt her recent actions were responsible for the bitter dissension. What does <u>dissension</u> mean? _____

5.   What do we mean by the right of political <u>dissent</u>? _____

_____

6.   The poem is a moving depiction of the _____ he felt upon first hearing of the birth of his son. (justifiable tender feeling)

7.   Mr. Langtry was realistic and matter-of-fact, and he thought anyone who would waste tears on a dilapidated old cabin in the hills was guilty of foolishness or _____ or both. (exaggerated emotional feeling)

8.   Acting on his _____, the foreman ordered the men out of the structure just minutes before it collapsed. ("feeling beforehand")

Answers to Self-Test

1. sensuous 2. sensory 3. devoting too much time to the pleasure of the senses 4. quarreling or hard feeling about differences of opinion 5. the right to disagree politically 6. sentiment 7. sentimentality 8. presentiment

29   SPEC, SPIC, look

Derivatives:

aspect (ASS spekt)
circumspect (SIR kum spekt)
inspect (in SPEKT)
introspection (in tro SPEK shun)
perspective (per SPEK tiv)

prospect (PRAH spekt)
retrospect (REH truh spekt)
spectacles (SPEK tuh kuhls)
spectre (SPEK ter)
spectrum (SPEK trum)

Prefixes
as (ad)—to, toward
circum—around
in—in, into
intro—within
per—complete,
    thorough
pro—forward
retro—backward

Suffixes
ion—act of
ive—that which
re—that which
rum—that which

inspects
  in—in
  spect—look

She always _____ my room first.
(looks in)

He sat in his cell for hours regretting his life in ret-

the act of looking
backward
  retro—backward
  spect—look

rospect. What does <u>retrospect</u> mean? _____

_____

Imprisonment had forced him into serious introspection, and he vowed to change himself for the better.

act of looking
within
  intro—within
  spect—look

What does <u>introspection</u> mean? _____

_____

circumspect

Tim is usually _____ in his
choice of friends. ("marked by looking around")

It would help you understand this problem if you would

perspective

look at it from the _____ of a
psychologist. (viewpoint; complete look)

prospect

We are faced with the _____ of
higher prices. ("look forward")

aspects
  a—toward
  spec—look

There are many _____ of the prob-
lem to consider. ("ways of looking toward")

looking-glasses

Granny left her spectacles on the wash basin. <u>Spec-
tacles</u> are: looking-glasses/false teeth/bracelets.

looked

Rugs available in a full <u>spectrum</u> of colors are a-
vailable in a wide range of things to be _____
at or seen.

spectre

A <u>spectre</u> is a ghost, a thing seen in the mind. The
Western world is still haunted by the _____
of nuclear destruction.

Self-Test

1. The Higbys were totally unaware of the legal _____ of the
    matter. ("ways of looking toward")

2. In _____ the trip seemed much more pleasur-
    able than it had actually been. (act of looking backward)

3. He was sorely tormented by the spectre of his guilt. What does <u>spectre</u>
    mean? _____

4. Freedom should give one the fullest spectrum of choice possible. A <u>spec-</u>
    <u>trum</u> refers to _____.

5. His answers to the detective's questions were always polite, always ____
    _____. (marked by looking around; careful)

6. Thrilled by the _____ of a fishing trip with his dad,
    Larry got out of bed the minute he was awakened. ("look forward")

7. You are not looking at your problems from the right perspective. What
    does <u>perspective</u> mean? _____

8. The long illness forced him into some painful but necessary introspection.
    <u>Introspection</u> is the act of _____.

Answers to Self-Test

1. aspects 2. retrospect 3. something seen in the mind 4. the entire range
of something 5. circumspect 6. prospect 7. viewpoint; complete look at
something 8. looking within

(30)   SPIR, breathe

Derivatives:

aspire (uh SPIRE)
conspire (kun SPIRE)
dispirited (dis SPIR uh tuhd)
expire (ik SPIRE)
inspire (in SPIRE)

perspire (per SPIRE)
respiration (res per AY shun)
spirited (SPIR uh tuhd)
spirometer (spir OM uh ter)

Prefixes
as (ad)—to, toward
con—with, together
dis—apart
ex—out
in—in
per—through
re—again

Other roots
meter—that which
    measures

Suffixes
ation—act of

"breathe out"
  ex—out
  spir—breathe

Expire literally means to _____.
Often expire means to breathe out for the last time,
or die. If a license of some sort is about to run out,

expire

it, too, is said to _____.

inspire
  in—in
  spir—breathe

To "breathe" courage into someone is to _____
courage.

Think of people "breathing together" in dark corners
to plot evil or harm against somebody else and you

conspire
  con—together
  spir—breathe

will have a vivid reference for the verb _____

_____.

Aspire means "breathe toward." Eliza Doolittle
aspired to be a great lady. Here aspired means:
gave up trying/earnestly desired.

earnestly desired

A doctor measures your rate of respiration, which
means your rate of: giving off moisture/inhaling and
exhaling air.

inhaling and
exhaling air

perspire

To "breathe through" the skin is to _____.

lively

Since "breath" and "life" are almost synonymous for
human beings, a spirited discussion would be: lively/
unnecessary.

A setback or defeat of some kind leaves most people

lacking spirit;
discouraged

feeling dispirited. What does dispirited mean? ____

_____

A spirometer is an instrument for measuring what?

breathing; lung
capacity

_____

Self-Test

1. This contract and its provisions will expire in six months. That is, in
    six months the contract will: begin/be reactivated/die.

2. The athletic commission believed that the coach and two of his players had _____ to lose the game. ("breathed together")

3. Secretly he aspired to be president of the country. <u>Aspired</u> means _____

_____.

4. When sales continued to drop over an eight-week period, even the most optimistic merchants became _____. (discouraged)

5. They were having a spirited conversation about the merits of domestic cars versus foreign cars. <u>Spirited</u> means _____.

6. The effects of emphysema were checked by weekly tests made by using a

_____. (instrument for measuring lung capacity)

7. If we say that a patient's <u>respiration</u> is irregular, what do we mean?

_____

Answers to Self-Test

1. die 2. conspired 3. desired or hoped; "breathed toward" 4. dispirited
5. lively 6. spirometer 7. that his rate of inhaling and exhaling is irregular

(31)   SOLV, SOLUT, free, loosen

Derivatives:

absolute (AB suh lute)   dissolve (dih ZOLV)
absolution (ab suh LEW shun)   insolvent (in SOL vunt)
absolve (ab ZOLV)   resolution (rez uh LEW shun)
dissolute (DIS suh lute)   resolve (ree ZOLV)
dissolution (dis suh LEW shun) solvent (SOL vunt)

Prefixes   Suffixes
ab—from, away   ion—act of
dis—apart   ent—being
in—not
re—again

                A business that is free of debt or that can pay its
solvent   debts readily is _____ (being free).
  solv—free
  ent—being   If you are temporarily out of money, you can say—

insolvent   euphemistically—that you are _____.
                (not free)

brought to
an end
  dis—apart
  solv—free

A relationship that is <u>dissolved</u> is: brought to an end/firmed up.

dissolute

People who are loose in morals or conduct are said

to be _____. ("loosened apart")
Overindulgence in food, drink, and the like is called

dissolution

_____. (act of loosening apart)

free from
  ab—from
  solv—free

A man is absolved of guilt feelings by confessing his sins to a priest. <u>Absolve</u> means to _____

_____. Upon his confession, the

absolution

priest gives the man _____.
(the act of freeing from)

free from

If you have <u>absolute</u> authority or power, you are: (under/free from) the influence or control of someone else.

you determine
to get one

<u>Resolve</u> literally means "free again," usually to free yourself from doubt. If you <u>resolve</u> to get a college education, what do you do? _____

_____

resolution

When an organization determines to do some special thing, such as trying to save an old landmark from the bulldozer, it puts its determination on record by

passing a _____.

Self-Test

1. He entered the little church, seeking absolution for his evil thoughts and deeds. What is <u>absolution</u>? _____

2. For two years he lived a dissolute life, wandering around the country aimlessly and occasionally working as a carnival roustabout. <u>Dissolute</u> means

_____

3. The firm is _____ and will soon go bankrupt. (not free from debt)

4. After the military takeover, Diego was made head of the provisional government and given _____ power. He quickly made himself into a dictator. (free from the influence or control of someone else)

5. The conservation club quickly passed a _____ to request the governor to withhold his endorsement of the proposed new dam. (determination)

6. After the accident in which his friend was killed, he was never to feel

_____ of guilt. (freed from)

Answers to Self-Test

1. forgiveness; act of being freed from guilt 2. loose in morals or conduct; "loosening apart" 3. insolvent 4. absolute 5. resolution 6. absolved

(32)   TEMPOR, time

Derivatives:
contemporaneous (kun temp er AY
    nee us)
contemporary (kun TEMP er air
    ee)
extemporaneous (eks temp er AY
    nee us)

pro tem (PRO TEM)
temporary (TEM per air ee)
tempo (TEM poe)
temporize (TEM per ize)

Prefixes
con—with, together
ex—out of, outside
pro—for

Suffixes
ary—one who
ary—relating to
eous—characterized by being
ize—verb ending

time
  tempor—time
  ary—related to

A temporary job lasts for only a limited _____.

If you temporize about a decision, you delay in mak-

time

ing it; you use up _____ in pointless or needless discussion.

The literal meaning of extemporaneous is "being out of time." Give a more current definition of it as it occurs in the following sentence: The chairman called on me to give a three-minute extemporaneous presentation of the reason why Smith Construction Company should merge with Western Factors.

not having time
to prepare ahead;
speaking "off the
cuff" as you go
along

_____

_____

You and the people of your own age are contempor- aries. Contemporaries literally means those

"together in time"   "_____."
  con—together
  tempor—time
  ary—one who

were not   George Washington and John Kennedy (were/were
                    not) contemporaries. Authors presently living or
                    alive in the past twenty or thirty years would be in-

contemporary   cluded in a course in _____
                    literature. ("together in time" with you)

                    If they are held in the same period of time, would a
                    horse show and a music festival be <u>contemporaneous</u>

yes   events? _____

                    If <u>pro</u> means "for," what is a chairman <u>pro tem</u>?

someone who serves _____
"for the time being"
                    An orchestra leader plays a well-known composition
                    at a much faster tempo than usual. What do you think

the time or rate   <u>tempo</u> means in this context? _____
of movement of the
music; the rhythm   _____

Self-Test

1. In the early days of his administration President Lincoln was not highly

    regarded by many of his _____. (those of
    approximately the same age; those "together in time")

2. Three times Sir Gawain asked the king to send help to the Gauls, and three

    times the king temporized. What does <u>temporized</u> mean? _____

    _____

3. While Mr. Kirsten is away on a trip, Miss Spencer is president pro tem.

    <u>Pro tem</u> means _____.

4. In some backward areas the _____ of life is still
    leisurely and graceful. (time; rhythm)

5. His _____ speeches about international finance
    are more interesting than his formal addresses. (marked by being with-
    out time to prepare; off the cuff)

6. The dance concert, the art exhibit, and the play are being scheduled as
    <u>contemporaneous</u> events. That is, the events are scheduled to occur

    _____.

Answers to Self-Test

1. contemporaries 2. stalled for time; engaged in pointless discussion
3. for the time being 4. tempo 5. extemporaneous 6. in the same period
of time

 TORT, twist

Derivatives:

contortion (kun TOR shun)	retort (ree TORT)
contortionist (kun TOR shun ist)	torture (TOR chure)
distort (dis TORT)	tortuous (TOR chew us)
extort (eks TORT)	torturous (TOR cher us)
extortion (eks TOR shun)	

Prefixes	Suffixes
con—together	ion—act of
dis—apart	ist—one who
ex—out of	ure—act of
re—back	ous—marked by

During the Middle Ages confessions were often obtained through <u>torture</u>, such as putting a man on the rack. How was pain inflicted on the body? _____

by twisting it
out of shape
 tort—twist
 ure—act of

_____

distort

It is usually unwise to _____ the truth. ("twist apart")

<u>Retort</u> means "to twist back." Give the current meaning in this sentence: "You're just as lazy as I am!"

to reply sharply;
to return in kind

she <u>retorted</u>. _____

_____

Gene went through all kinds of contortions as he tried to get through the tiny open window. What does <u>con-tortion</u> mean? _____

twisting the body
parts together
 con—together
 tort—twist
 ion—act of

_____

contortionist

A person who entertains others by unusual or difficult "twistings" of the body is called a _____

_____ .

Criminals often try to extort money from people.

"twist out"
 ex—out
 tort—twist

Extort literally means to "_____."

extortion

There are laws against such acts of _____

_____.

Two adjectives sharing the root tort are sometimes confused. A tortuous road is full of twists and turns; a torturous illness is cruelly painful. Building the

torturous

pyramids was _____ work for the

tortuous

slaves. The winding path up the hill is _____

_____.

Self-Test

1. It was clear that the elderly housekeeper and her husband had not kidnapped the child and had not meant to extort money from his parents.

    What does extort mean? _____

2. It was _____ work having to pull the sled by hand. (cruelly painful)

3. Even wild sheep would have had trouble in following that _____ mountain path. (twisting; winding)

4. We could tell he was suffering by the _____ of his face. (twistings together; grimaces)

5. It would take a contortionist to get into a car that small! What is a contortionist? _____

6. "My mother may be limited, as you say, but at least she doesn't brag about her ignorance!" Liz _____. (replied quickly or sharply; returned in kind)

Answers to Self-Test

1. to "twist out"; demand 2. torturous 3. tortuous 4. contortions 5. one who is a professional at putting the body into odd or unusual positions 6. retorted

34   VID, VIS, see, look

Derivatives:

advise (ad VIZE)
improvise (IM pro vize)
improvisation (im prahv uh ZAY shun)
improviser (IM pruh vize er)
invidious (in VID ee us)

providence (PRAHV uh dunss)
providentially (prahv uh DEN shul lee)
revise (ree VIZE)
supervise (SOO per vize)

Prefixes
ad—to, toward
im—not
in—not
pro—forward
re—again
super—over

Suffixes
ence—act of
er—one who
ation—act of
ally—adverb; manner

You "look toward"
his problem.
  ad—toward
  vise—look

What do you do when you <u>advise</u> someone? _____

_____

"look again"
  re—again
  vise—look

If you <u>revise</u> your opinion about something, you
"_____."

overlook workers
to see they do their
work properly
  super—over
  vis—look
  or—one who

Keeping in mind the literal meaning, what is a <u>supervisor's</u> general function? To _____

_____.

A religious person often feels that God has taken an active role in causing things to happen: It was divine providence that the rain came just in time to save the crops. What does <u>providence</u> mean here literally?

the act of seeing
forward (ahead)
  pro—forward
  vid—see
  ence—act of

_____

providentially

If you feel something happens to you at just the right time, you can say that it happened _____

_____. (in the manner of providence)

A teacher is caught without time to prepare a test,

so when he arrives in class he has to <u>improvise</u>; that is, to make one up as he goes along. Literally, to <u>improvise</u> means to do something "not seeing forward (without looking ahead of time)." Music that is made up as the performer goes along is called

improvisation

_____. Most jazz musicians

improvisers

are good _____.

<u>Invidious</u> literally means "not seeing." An <u>invidious</u> remark is unfair or offensive. If you were to be compared with an especially talented or good-looking brother or sister, no doubt you would feel the com-

invidious

parison to be _____.

Self-Test

1. At the very last moment, just when it looked as though the show would not be able to open, financial support arrived _____ in the person of J. Morgan Warbucks. (just at the right time; in the manner of divine intervention)

2. Harley managed to _____ some music for the dance Marie was performing in the center of the living room. (make up music "without looking ahead")

3. Jeanne felt it was _____ to compare her to a woman twice her age. (unfair or offensive; "not seeing")

4. If you are a good enough musician to call yourself an <u>improviser</u>, what are you able to do? _____

Answers to Self-Test

1. providentially 2. improvise 3. invidious 4. to make up music as you play it

(35)   VOC, VOCAT, VOK, call, calling

Derivatives:

advocate (AD vuh kut)
avocation (av oh KAY shun)
convocation (kon voh KAY shun)
equivocate (ee QUIV oh kate)
invoke (in VOKE)

irrevocable (ir REV uh kuh buhl)
provoke (pruh VOKE)
revoke (ree VOKE)
vocal (VOE kuhl)
vocation (voe KAY shun)

Prefixes
ad—to, toward
a—not
con—with, together
in—on
ir—not
pro—forward, forth
re—back

Other roots
equi—equal

Suffixes
ate—one who
ation—act of
able—able

by speaking

A vocal protest is made: by speaking/in writing.

A drunk driver may find that his driver's license is

revoked
  re—back
  vok—call

_____ (called back).

An action or decision that can never be "called back"

irrevocable

is _____.

What does it mean to <u>provoke</u> a response from a

to call it forth
  pro—forward
  vok—call

friend? _____

In a special ceremony the Hopi Indians <u>invoke</u> the gods

They call on
the gods to
send rain.

to send rain. What do they do? _____

_____

recommends
  ad—toward
  voc—call
  ate—one who

Laura is an <u>advocate</u> of greater job opportunities for
women. She (recommends/objects to) greater opportunities for women.

When asked if he would devote time to helping with
the club activities, Mr. Wells seemed to say both
yes and no; in other words, he used double meanings
or misleading statements. The verb that means to

equivocate

put equal emphasis in opposed directions is _____

_____.

"calling"

A synonym for <u>vocation</u> is "_____."
What someone does with his leisure time is his hobby,

avocation

or _____. ("not the calling")

In college a calling together of students is usually

convocation

called a _____rather than an
assembly.

Self-Test

1. His action seemed as irrevocable as dropping a letter into a mailbox.
    What does <u>irrevocable</u> mean? _____

2. Mrs. Hawkins knew exactly how to approach the problem: she would in-
    voke the help of the mayor and the town council. <u>Invoke</u> means to _____
    _____.

3. Jane was irritated. "Really, John! Why must you _____
    even about a simple thing like where we are going on our vacation?"
    (speak with equal emphasis in opposite directions)

4. Although I make my living by raising greenhouse plants, my _____
    is playing a jazz saxophone.

5. Professor Greene is an advocate of world federalism. What is an <u>advo-</u>
    <u>cate</u>? _____

6. The new student body regulations will be discussed in a _____
    to be held at eleven o'clock this morning. (meeting; assembly)

7. The Motor Vehicle Bureau threatened to revoke my driver's license. What
    does <u>revoke</u> mean? _____

Answers to Self-Test

1. not able to be recalled 2. "call on" 3. equivocate 4. avocation
5. a supporter; one who "calls toward" 6. convocation 7. "to call back"

Now that you've mastered this chapter, you might enjoy a new look at the drawing that opens it on page 88.

ANTEHILL

SUBSMASH

INTERDISHES

PRETYPEWRITER

CHAPTER FIVE
Latin Prefixes

(1)   AB-, ABS-, from, away

Derivatives:

abduct (ab DUKT)

aberrant (AB er unt)

abnormal (ab NOR muhl)

aborigine (ab er IJ juhn ee)

abrade (uh BRADE)

absolve (ab ZOLVE)

absolution (ab so LOO shun)

abstain (ab STAIN)

abstinence (AB stin unce)

Roots

err—wander

duct—lead

rad—scrape

solve—free, loosen

tain, tin—hold

Suffixes

ant—marked by

ence—act of

ion—act of

abnormal

If your temperature is much higher or lower than

normal, it is _____.

A person who is kidnapped is abducted, which liter-

"led away"

ab—away

duct—lead

ally means "_____."

from

Aborigines are primitive people who have existed

_____ the beginning (origin).

In the course of an investigation, a man has been ab-

He has been freed

from guilt.

solved of guilt. What has been done to him? _____

_____

In some religions a person who confesses his sins is

freedom from

guilt (forgiveness)

given absolution. What is he given? _____

_____

aberrant	What adjective describes the behavior of a man who wanders from the right or usual path? _____ behavior
"speaks away" ab—away dic—speak	An aging king decides to abdicate. He gives up his throne or authority. Literally he "_____ _____ " his authority, usually in a public ceremony.
abraded	The walls of a canyon are gradually _____ by dust storms and muddy water. ("scraped away")
hold away from it	If you abstain from some activity, such as smoking or drinking, you: participate in it/hold away from it. Members of a religious order who hold away from
abstinence	sexual activity are said to practice _____. (act of holding away)

Self-Test

1. The Australian bushmen, who live today much as men did in the Stone Age, are _____. (from the beginning)

2. Once he had been _____ of blame for the accident, he felt much better. (freed from)

3. The brothers in a religious order must take a vow of _____ _____. (holding away)

4. The instructor forced the frog to ingest some alcohol and then asked us to observe any aberrant patterns of behavior it manifested. Aberrant means
_____

5. If the marble exterior of an old building has been badly abraded, what has happened to it? _____

Answers to Self-Test

1. aborigines 2. absolved 3. abstinence 4. "wandering from" the usual pattern 5. it has been scraped, or worn, away; it has lost its smoothness

(2)   AD-, to, toward

Derivatives:
adjoining (uh JOIN ing)   annotated (AN uh tate uhd)
adore (uh DORE)   assimilation (uh sim uh LAY shun)
aggravate (AG gruh vate)   attract (uh TRAKT)
allocate (AL uh kate)

Roots
grav—serious,
        worse
loc—place
orare—pray
simil—like
tract—draw
vis—look, see

Suffixes
ate—verb ending
ation—act of
ing—current act of

adjoining

Rooms in a hotel that are literally "joined to" each other are _____ rooms.

advises
  ad—toward
  vis—look

A faculty advisor who "looks toward" solutions for your problems _____ you.

to worship
("pray to") or
highly regard him

If orare means "pray," what does it mean to adore a hero? _____

affect

When ad- is added to a root like range, the d turns into r: ad + range becomes arrange. (Say adrange out loud five or six times as rapidly as possible and you will see what happens. You will also gain an idea of why pronunciation and spelling gradually change over the years.) What does ad + fect become?

_____ The process whereby the d of the prefix ad- turns into the same consonant as the one following it is called assimilation, "the act of becoming similar to" something else. The word assim-ilation is an example of the very thing it defines: ad + similation becomes assimilation. Because of the

assimilation

principle of _____ , the prefix ad- sometimes becomes af-, ag-, al-, am-, an-, ap-, ar-, or as-.

attracts
  at—toward
  tract—draw

Tract = draw. What does honey do to flies? It ____ _____ them.

aggravate it

Grave = serious, worse. Scratching may do what to a skin infection? _____

allocates
  al—toward
  loc—place

Loc = place. The Federal Government _____ a great deal of money for military expenditures.

annotated

A biography containing explanatory notes or comments is called an _____ biography.

It is interesting to note that <u>assimilation</u> also applies to the way in which immigrant people are brought into the mainstream of American culture. They quickly become similar to other Americans, and this proc-

assimilation   ess is called _____.

Self-Test

1.   Each city must _____ a large sum of money for its transportation system.   ("place toward")

2.   Speaking to your father when you are angry will only aggravate an already tense situation. <u>Aggravate</u> means _____.

3.   An <u>annotated</u> biography contains _____.

4.   When added to the root <u>range</u>, the prefix <u>ad-</u> becomes <u>ar-</u> (<u>arrange</u>). This process is called _____.

5.   If you treat someone as though he were a god—that is, if you worship him— you _____ him.

Answers to Self-Test

1. allocate 2. worsen; make more serious 3. explanatory notes or comments
4. assimilation 5. adore

③   ANTE-, before

Derivatives:
  antebellum (ant ee BELL um)   antediluvian (an tuh duh LOO vee un)
  antecedents (an tuh SEED unts)   anterior (an TEER ee er)
  antedate (AN tuh date)   anteroom (AN tee room)

Roots	Suffixes
bell—war	ent—one who
ced—go	ian—characterized by being
diluv—flood	um—characterized by being

Your <u>antecedents</u> would be the family members that

before   "go _____" you; in other words, your ancestors.

World War I <u>antedated</u> World War II; that is, it

happened ("dated")
before it   _____ it.

A waiting room that leads to a larger room can also

anteroom	be called an _____. ("before room")
front	An <u>anterior</u> view of something is a: (back/front) view.
	<u>Bell</u> means "war." The South before the Civil War
Antebellum (used here as a proper noun)	is called the _____ South.
	If <u>diluv</u> refers to the great flood (deluge) reported in the Old Testament, what would <u>antediluvian</u> mean?
before the flood	_____
	If you wish to exaggerate, you can describe something
antediluvian	very old as being _____. (existing before the flood)

Self-Test

1. The famous novel <u>Gone with the Wind</u> begins in the Antebellum South. What does <u>antebellum</u> mean? _____

2. To fifteen-year-old Catherine the principal's attitude about student attire seemed _____. (existing before the great flood; very old)

3. The brain tumor was located in the <u>anterior</u> lobe of the brain. Which lobe is that? front/rear/center.

4. My antecedents were farmers who lived in Wales. What are <u>antecedents</u>?

    _____

5. Lady Margery heard the two ladies chattering away in the _____ _____. (waiting room; "room before")

6. My birthday is in June, while yours is in August; so mine _____ yours by two months. (dates before)

Answers to Self-Test

1. before the war (in this case, the Civil War) 2. antediluvian 3. the front lobe 4. ancestors; people who came before 5. anteroom 6. antedates

④ CIRCUM-, around

Derivatives:
circumference (sir KUM frunce)
circumlocution (sir kum low KEW shun)
circumnavigate (sir kum NAV uh gate)
circumspect (SIR kum spekt)
circumvent (SIR kum vent)

Roots   Suffixes
fer—carry   ate—verb ending
ig—go, carry on   ence—result of
locut—speak   ion—act of
nav—ship
vent—come

The circumference of a circle is the line that could

around   be "carried _____" its outer edge.

Navigate means "to make a ship to go." A luxury

circumnavigating   liner offers an enjoyable way of _____
the earth. (making a ship go around)

To avoid trouble by coming (going) around a problem

circumvent   is to _____ trouble.

If you are circumspect in your choice of friends, you

look around   "_____" carefully in order
  circum—around   to act wisely.
  spect—look

If you ask a question of a politician and he responds
with a circumlocution, does he come to the point?

No   _____

around   (He talks all _____ the point.)

Self-Test

1. By apologizing to Ed, Martin hoped to _____ further
unpleasantness. (go around; avoid)

2. Recognizing the importance of their visit, the two husbands tried to be as
_____ as possible in answering their wives'
questions. (careful)

3. According to the news writeup, he planned to circumnavigate the world in
a rowboat. What did he plan to do? _____

4. After measuring it, Hank said the _____ of the
of the circle was 12.60 feet. (distance around)

5. A person who uses circumlocutions is probably trying to: build up inter-
est/avoid an issue.

Answers to Self-Test

1. circumvent 2. circumspect 3. travel around; go around the world in a
rowboat 4. circumference 5. avoid an issue

(5)   COM-, CON- COL-, CO-, with, together

Derivatives:
    collaborate (kuh LAB er ate)   conjugal (KON juh guhl)
    combine (KOM bine)   coordinate (koe ORD in ate)
    commingle (kum MING uhl)   cooperate (koe OP er ate)
    complaisant (kum PLAY sunt)   incongruity (in kun GREW uh tee)
    congruent (kun GREW unt)

Roots	Suffixes
bin—bind	al—marked by
gru—agree	ant—characterized by being
jug—yoke	ate—verb ending
plais—please	ent—marked by
	in—not
	ity—state of

The prefix com- is usually used before roots beginning with b, p, or m. A person who is obliging or

complaisant   gracious or courteous is a _____
  com—with   person. ("pleasing with")
  plais—please
  ant—being

If many people mingle together in a crowd, they are

commingle   said to _____.

A group of persons joined or bound together for business or political gain, usually underhanded, is called

combine   a _____. As a verb, combine

together   means literally "to bind things _____."

The prefix col- is used before roots beginning with l.
Thus, to labor with someone else on a project is to

collaborate   _____.

The prefix co- is used before roots beginning with o.

cooperate   To operate together in some fashion is to _____

_____.

If the activities of two groups are coordinated, they

together   are regulated _____.

Most other roots take the prefix con-. Being married
establishes a conjugal relationship between a man and

"yoked together"   a woman; they are then "_____."
  con—together
  jug—yoke

conjugal	Happy married people refer to their state as _____ _____ bliss.
	If <u>gru</u> means "agree," then two opinions that are
congruent con—with gru—agree	harmonious are _____ opinions.
	The <u>incongruity</u> of a man's stated beliefs and his actions would mean what? _____
that the beliefs and the actions did not agree with each other	_____

Self-Test

1. Lester felt lucky indeed; he had married a very complaisant woman.

    <u>Complaisant</u> means _____.

2. Their marriage could hardly be called a state of _____
    bliss. (marked by being yoked together)

3. Mr. Burke commented on the incongruity of our criticizing the British
    for the very qualities we most admire in them. <u>Incongruity</u> refers to

    _____.

4. At exactly six in the evening the townspeople poured into the streets and

    _____ excitedly. (mingled together)

5. The United Crusade is a coordinated attempt to raise funds for charitable

    organizations. <u>Coordinated</u> means _____.

6. The Attorney General placed the blame for the swindle on a Chicago ____
    _____. (group bound together usually for an under-
    handed purpose)

7. Although they came from radically different backgrounds, their views on

    the importance of conservation were _____. (marked
    by agreeing with each other)

Answers to Self-Test

1. obliging, gracious, "pleasing with" 2. conjugal 3. lack of agreement between stated beliefs and actions 4. commingled 5. regulated together 6. combine 7. congruent

(6)   COUNTER-, CONTRA-, CONTRO-, against, opposite

Derivatives:
    contraband (KON truh band)   controversy (KON truh verse ee)
    contralto (kuhn TRAHL toe)   counterclockwise (count er KLOK
    contrary (KON trair ee)   wise)
    contrariness (kuhn TRAIR ee nuss)   countermand (count er MAND)
    contravene (kon truh VEEN)

Roots

band—ban
mand—order
ven—come (go)
vers—turn

Suffixes

ness—quality of
y—act of

against, opposite

If you move the hands of a clock in a counterclockwise
fashion, you move them backwards, or _____
_____ their usual direction of movement.

If a junior officer's order to his men is countermanded by a senior officer, what happens to the junior officer's order? _____

It is cancelled.
  counter—against
  mand—order

An individual who is contrary always seems to get

opposite, against

pleasure in taking a(n) _____ view
of things. He often irritates others because of this

contrariness

_____.

Smuggled goods are brought in "against a ban" and

contraband

thus can be called _____.

A female whose voice is lower than that of an alto is

contralto

classified as a _____. ("opposite
of an alto") A contralto is the lowest woman's voice.

against, opposite

In a controversy people are turned _____
each other in attitudes or opinions.

If a person or group contravenes, does it keep to the

go against it

law or go against it? _____

Self-Test

1. Michael's _____ prevented him from becoming a
    really successful consultant. (habit of taking the opposite view)

2. The new environmental protection law was <u>contravened</u> by two groups of developers. The law was _____.

3. The Captain _____ the order given by Lieutenant Jones. (cancelled; reversed)

4. When the caller gives the signal, the square dancers move in a <u>counter-clockwise</u> direction. How do they move? _____

    _____

5. The Border Patrol seized twenty boxes of watches and other contraband. What is <u>contraband</u>? _____

6. The duet was sung by an alto and a _____. (the lowest woman's voice)

Answers to Self-Test

1. contrariness 2. set aside; ignored; gone against 3. countermanded
4. in reverse; opposite to the direction in which the hands of a clock move
5. goods smuggled or brought in "against the ban" 6. contralto

(7)   DE-, down, away

Derivatives:
decelerate (dee CELL er ate)   depress (dee PRESS)
demote (dee MOTE)   descend (dee SEND)
depose (dee POSE)   detonate (DET uh nate)
depredation (dep ruh DAY shun)   devaluate (dee VAL yoo ate)

Roots   Suffixes
celer—quickness,   ate—verb ending
       speed   ation—act of
mot—move
pos—put, place
pred—prey, plunder
scend—climb

<u>Depress</u>, <u>descend</u>, and <u>devaluate</u> all share the prefix

de   _____ meaning "down." Complete the literal meanings of these words:

press down   depress = to _____

climb down   descend = to _____

take down or   devaluate = to _____
lessen in value

They put him off
the throne; remove
him from office.

The people <u>depose</u> their king. If <u>pos</u> means "put or place," what do they do to him? _____

deposed

Any person who is removed from an office or power can also be said to be _____ .
("placed down")

demote

To promote a person is to move him forward; to move him down is to _____ him.

decelerate

To accelerate is to speed up (literally, "speed toward"); to slow down is to _____ .

depredations

<u>Depredation</u> is an act of making away with plunder, loot, or booty. If a housewife wishes to joke about her husband's and children's raids on the cookie jar, she can refer to these raids as _____ .

detonated

Occasionally <u>de</u> is used merely to intensify the meaning of the root to which it is attached. Thus, <u>detonate</u>, which means to set off an explosion, is derived from <u>ton</u> (thunder) and means "to make a very thundering sound." We took cover before the dynamite was _____ .

Self–Test

1. He ran the car off the road because he realized there was not time to _____ . (slow down)

2. The sheepherders were alarmed by the depredations of what they assumed was a wolf pack. What are <u>depredations</u>? _____

3. The king was dethroned in 1742 and a dictator came to power. Two years later the dictator was in turn deposed by a powerful group of nobles. <u>Deposed</u> means _____ .

4. In an attempt to curtail inflation, the government attempted to _____ gold. (lessen in value)

5. He _____ the dynamite before all of us could find cover. (set off the explosion)

6. It was merely a measure of economy that forced Mr. Pettus to demote one of the junior officers of the company. <u>Demote</u> means _____ .

Answers to Self-Test

1. decelerate 2. raids for loot or plunder 3. removed from office; placed down 4. devaluate 5. detonated 6. to move down; to move to a lesser position

 8 DIS-, DIF-, DI, apart, not

Derivatives:

diffident (DIF uh dunt)	disparage (dis PEAR ij)
digress (deye GRESS)	disparity (dis PEAR uh tee)
discomfiture (dis KUM fuh chure)	disrupt (dis RUPT)
disconsolate (dis KON suh luht)	dissenting (dis SENT ing)
disjoint (dis JOINT)	

Roots
comfit—comfort,
       fitting together
consol—comfort,
       cheer
fid—faith
gress—step, go
par—equal
rupt—break
sent—feel

Suffixes
ate—marked by
age—verb ending
ent—marked by
ity—state of
ure—state of

disrupt
  dis—apart
  rupt—break

To break (rupt) apart a class is to _____ it.

disjoint

To take a chicken apart at the joints is to _____ it.

disagrees

John casts the only dissenting vote at a meeting. If sent means "feel," John: (agrees/disagrees) with the group.

not

The prefix dis- can also mean "not." A disparity in the ages of two people would mean they were _____ equal in years. Disparage originally meant to marry someone of lower rank. Today it means to belittle someone or something as not equal or not worthy.

dis

What part of the word disparage means not? _____

diffident

The prefix dif- is used before a root beginning with an f. A person who is shy, who has no self-confidence, is said to be _____. (apart from faith in himself)

To console a person is to give him comfort or cheer.

too sad to be cheered up | If he is <u>disconsolate</u>, then he is _____ _____.

Revealing someone's foolishness or error in front of a group may lead to his discomfiture. <u>Discomfiture</u>

embarrassment, lack of poise | means _____

<u>Gress</u> means "step." What does a lecturer do when

He gets off into another topic. | he <u>digresses</u> from his stated topic? _____

Self-Test

1. Sam was too diffident a person to become very popular. What does <u>diffident</u> mean? _____

2. Mrs. Greene tried to keep on the subject of the club's finances, but several of the ladies seemed determined to make her _____.

3. Reporters were quick to detect a disparity in the two government press releases. <u>Disparity</u> means _____.

4. Mr. Sims had a nasty habit of _____ both his wife and her cooking. (belittling as not worthy)

5. Rinda felt _____ after losing the contest. (unable to be consoled)

6. Noticing my discomfiture, the hostess came over and rescued me from Mrs. Sanborn. What is <u>discomfiture</u>? _____

7. Senator Thomas was the only _____ member of the committee. (disagreeing)

Answers to Self-Test

1. shy, lacking confidence, "apart from faith" in himself 2. digress 3. lack of equality, imbalance 4. disparaging 5. disconsolate 6. embarrassment, loss of poise 7. dissenting

(9) EX-, EF-, E-, out

Derivatives:
exempt (egg ZEMPT)   excise (eks SIZE)
efface (uh FACE)   exclude (eks KLUDE)
efficacy (EF fuh kuh see)   exhale (eks HALE)

Derivatives (continued):
    eject (ee JEKT)   expel (eks PELL)
    eradicate (ee RAD uh kate)   exposé (eks poe ZAY)

Roots   Suffixes
cis—cut   acy—quality of
clud—shut   ate—verb ending
emp—choose
fic—do, make, carry on
hale—breathe
ject—throw
pel—drive
pos—put, place
rad—root

out

Exclude, expel, and exhale all share the prefix ex-,
meaning _____. Complete the literal
meaning of these words:

shut out

exclude = to _____

drive out

expel = to _____

breathe out

exhale = to _____

A surgeon decides to cut out someone's appendix; in
his report he will say he _____ the
appendix.

excised
   ex—out
   cis—cut

Lena's brother was exempted from jury duty. Even
though you did not know that emp means "choose,"
you would know that he: (did/did not) have to serve

did not

on a jury. The answer comes from the prefix _____,

ex-

meaning _____.

out

Fic means "do, make, carry on." To increase the
efficacy of this medicine, shake it vigorously before
using. Efficacy means: the purity of the product/the
ability to carry out the desired function.

the ability to
carry out the
desired function
   ef—out
   fic—do, carry on

A headline read, "Exposé of Mafia." Literally exposé is "an act of putting something _____" for
public attention. Usually an exposé is an act of showing up some crime or dishonesty.

out

A person who tries to keep himself from standing out
or being noticed (he "faces out or away" from others)

self-effacing

is self-_____ing. In other words, he is extremely modest. <u>Efface</u> can have a stronger meaning. To rewrite a passage so that you efface its meaning is to wipe it out or obliterate it.

If <u>rad</u> means "root," what does it mean to <u>eradicate</u>

to pull them out by the roots; get rid of them

weeds? To _____

The protesters were <u>ejected</u> from the hall. If <u>ject</u>

They were thrown out.

means "throw," what was done to them? _____

_____

Self-Test

1. Using distilled water increases the efficacy of this product. What does <u>efficacy</u> mean? _____

2. In spite of his outstanding achievements in science, Dr. Edgars has remained a self-effacing man. <u>Self-effacing</u> means _____

_____.

3. Three top officials of the company were named in the newspaper's black-market _____. (act of showing up some crime or dishonesty)

4. Because of his disability, he was _____ from taking physical education. ("chosen out"; freed from)

5. Providing meaningful jobs for more people is the most desirable means of _____ poverty. (getting rid of; pulling out by the roots)

6. A team of surgeons found and _____ a large tumor in her abdomen. (cut out)

Answers to Self-Test

1. the ability of a product to carry out its desired function 2. very modest
3. exposé 4. exempted 5. eradicating 6. excised

(10) INTER-, between

Derivatives:
  interject (in ter JEKT)
  interlocutory (in ter LOK yuh tore ee)
  intermittent (in ter MITT unt)

  interracial (in ter RAY shuhl)
  interregnum (in ter REGG num)
  interstate (IN ter state)

Roots
mit—send
reg—king

off and on

between

temporary

Suffixes
ent—marked by
ory—based on

An <u>interstate</u> trucking firm is a firm that operates

between   _____ states.

A marriage between two people of different racial

interracial   origins is an _____ marriage.

If <u>reg</u> means "king," what do you think an <u>interregnum</u>

a period of time   is? _____
between kings
when no one is
on the throne   _____

<u>Intermittent</u> rains are "sent between" periods of no
rain. Thus, <u>continuous</u> rain would mean rain that
falls over a long period of time, while <u>intermittent</u>
rains would fall: heavily/off and on.

<u>Ject</u> means "throw." If you <u>interject</u> a remark into

a conversation, you throw it _____
the speech of others. If you cannot get a word in
edgewise, you may have to <u>interject</u> it!

John and Mary received an <u>interlocutory</u> decree of
divorce. If <u>locut</u> means "speech or conversation,"
the decree is made while they are still suing each
each other for divorce and is therefore: temporary/
lasting. Eventually it will be followed by a final decree of divorce.

Self-Test

1. His once-famous memory was impaired by intermittent periods of forget-

    fulness. Intermittent means _____.

2. King Henry died and left no heir. The powerful nobles could not agree
    among themselves on a successor. During the interregnum the country
    was ruled by Henry's mistress, almost the only person in the court that

    everyone felt no fear of. What does <u>interregnum</u> mean? _____

    _____.

3. They were so absorbed in their conversation that he could _____
    only a few words. ("throw between")

4. That license has to be approved by the _____ Commerce
    Commission. ("between states")

5. Mr. Adams asked for an interlocutory decree of divorce from Mildred.

Interlocutory means _____

_____ .

6. The new condominium has achieved what its planners hoped it would a-

chieve—not just desegregation but _____ harmony.
("between races")

Answers to Self-Test

1. off and on; occurring from time to time 2. the time between kings 3. interject 4. Interstate 5. temporary decree granted while a divorce case is pending 6. interracial

(11) INTRA-, INTRO-, within

Derivatives:
intramural (in truh MURE uhl)   intravenously (in truh VEE nuss lee)
intrastate (in truh STATE)   introvert (IN truh vert)
introspection (in truh SPEK shun)   introversion (IN truh ver zhun)
intravenous (in truh VEE nuss)

Roots	Suffixes
mural—walls (of a school)	al—relating to
	ion—act of
spect—look	ly—adverb ending; manner
ven—vein	
vert—turn	

Intermural athletic events are games between teams from different schools. Games that are played by

intramural   teams within the same school are _____ athletic events.

A trucking firm that is licensed to carry goods from one state to another is an interstate company. A firm that is limited to transporting goods within one state

intrastate   is an _____ company.

within   An intravenous injection is given _____ a vein. Patients who are unable to eat and assimilate

intravenously   food are given nourishment _____ . (adverb: in the vein)

"turns within"   An introvert is literally someone who _____
intro—within
vert—turn   _____ . An introvert

characteristically is more interested in his own thoughts and feelings than what is going on around

introversion

him. In general, _____ is the characteristic of preferring to think rather than to act. (act of turning within)

John's imprisonment brought about a long period of introspection. Literally, he engaged in the action of

"looking within"
intro—within
spec—look

_____; he examined his own experience and weighed it thoughtfully.

Self-Test

1. It was surprising that an _____ like Marie would marry an active, outgoing person like Judson. (one who turns within)

2. A faculty team will play against a student team in the first of this year's _____ activities. (within the same school)

3. The introspection forced on him by a long period of illness made a striking change in his personality. What does introspection mean? _____

_____

4. In the final stages of her illness Mrs. Strang had to be fed intravenously. That is, she was fed _____.

Answers to Self-Test

1. introvert 2. intramural 3. act of looking within, examining one's own experience 4. by injections in the vein

(12) OB-, OC-, OF-, OP-, against

Derivatives:
object (ub JEKT, OB jikt)   obstruct (ub STRUKT)
objective (ub JEKT iv)   obtuse (ub TOOSE)
obscure (ub SKURE)   occult (uh KULT)
obscurity (ub SKURE uh tee)   offend (uh FEND)
obstreperous (ub STREP er us)   oppose (uh POSE)

At our most primitive level of emotions, we might well throw something at a thing or person we did not like. The verb object retains some of that idea,

"throw against"
ob—against
ject—throw

since it literally means "to _____."
The noun object retains some of that idea, too: an object is something that can be thrown against. (An

objective is a target, something you aim at in throwing.)

blocks its way

Obstruct means "build against." A person who tries to obstruct justice: helps it along/blocks its way.

loud and disorderly; noisy and unruly

A speaker is plagued by an obstreperous group of pickets. If streper means "to make a noise," the pickets are being _____ _____ .

obscured

To obscure something is to put a cover against it and thus to darken it. Mr. Bell's choice of words _____ his meaning. (covered)

obscure

A poet who is little known (who is in the dark) is an _____ poet. Obscure sounds are

not distinct; hard to identify clearly

sounds that are _____ _____ . Robert became famous for writing one good play, then he quickly fell

obscurity

into _____ . (darkness; state of being covered against)

obtuse
 ob—against
 tuse—beat

Sometimes a person will appear so dull or stupid that you feel you would like to beat (tuse) against him to make him understand. Such a person is _____ _____ .

op-

Ob- added to the root pos forms the verb obpose. You should remember from an earlier discussion of assimilation what happens in a situation like this.

The ob- turns into _____ and the word becomes

oppose

_____ . Pos means "put"; thus, to

put yourself against him

oppose someone is to _____ .

to strike against someone or something

Fend means "strike." What is the literal meaning of offend? _____

occult

Occult comes from a Latin word occultus meaning "hidden" (Oc- + cult = cover against, cover up). Because it appears to be mysterious and requires knowledge hidden from the average person, astrology is sometimes called an _____ science.

Self-Test

1. Mrs. Pettigrew was too <u>obtuse</u> to see the point. That is, she was: too busy arguing/hard of hearing/dull and stupid.

2. He claimed to be a member of Sons of Satan, an _____ religious group that believes in and practices black magic. (hidden; requiring knowledge outside the laws of the natural world)

3. Normally Brenda has no trouble in babysitting for the Smiths, but last Saturday evening both Carl and Butch were obstreperous. What does

   obstreperous mean? _____

4. Lionel grew up in an _____ little town in Kansas. (not well known; in the dark)

5. The two motorcyclists swore they had done nothing to _____ the law. (build against; hinder)

Answers to Self-Test

1. dull and stupid 2. occult 3. noisy, disorderly 4. obscure 5. obstruct

(13)   PER-, through, thoroughly

Derivatives:

percolate (PER kuh late)	persecute (PER suh kute)
peremptory (per EM ter ee)	perspicacious (per spuh KAY shus)
perennial (per EN ee uhl)	perspicacity (per spuh KASS uh tee)
perforate (PER fer ate)	perspire (per SPIRE)
permeate (PER mee ate)	

Roots
col—drain
empt—choose
enn—year
forare—bore
meare—pass, go
secut—follow
spic—see
spir—breathe

Suffixes
ate—verb ending
ial—characterized by being
ious—marked by
ity—quality of
ory—marked by

perforate

What verb means "to bore through" (make a hole in) a piece of paper or cardboard? _____

perspire

<u>Spir</u> means "breathe." When you become very warm, you breathe through the skin, or _____.

As a ball player, Willie Mays is a <u>perennial</u> favorite.

If <u>enn</u> means "year," then <u>perennial</u> means lasting

through the years
  per—through
  enn—year

_____ .

<u>Permeate</u> means to pass through. If the odor of cab-

present
everywhere

bage <u>permeates</u> a house, it is: present everywhere/
apparent only in the kitchen.

In the kind of coffeepot known as a <u>percolator</u>, boiling

through

water drains _____ ground coffee.

<u>Persecute</u> literally means "to follow thoroughly" (to

punished again
and again

the end). A person who is <u>persecuted</u> is: made fam-
ous/punished again and again.

Uncle Oliver is keen in observing and understanding.

sees through
things
  per—through
  spic—see

He is <u>perspicacious</u>, which literally means he _____

_____ .

No one else in the family besides Uncle Oliver pos-

perspicacity

sesses such _____ . (quality of
seeing through things)

<u>Empt</u> means "choose." Your boss gives you a <u>per-</u>
<u>emptory</u> order to work overtime. Does he give you

No (he has
thoroughly
chosen for you)
  per—thoroughly
  empt—choose

a chance to refuse? _____

Self-Test

1. A feeling of patriotism seemed to _____ the crowd.
(pass through)

2. I was impressed with the perspicacity of his remarks about social welfare
programs. What does <u>perspicacity</u> mean? _____

_____

3. The fight ended at once when Father gave us a peremptory order to go up-
stairs. A <u>peremptory</u> order allows no room for _____

_____ .

4. A flowering plant that is a <u>perennial</u> lives: only one year/from year to
year.

5. Spiral notebook paper has a _____ edge so that it can easily be torn out. (bored through; containing holes)

6. After receiving the tenth traffic citation in a week, Hubert shook his head in dismay and said he thought the police were trying to _____ him. (punish again and again)

Answers to Self-Test

1. permeate 2. keenness of mind; ability to see through things 3. refusal or further choice 4. from year to year 5. perforated 6. persecute

(14) POST-, after

Derivatives:

postbellum (post BELL uhm)   postmortem (post MORT em)
posterior (poss TEER ee er)   postnatal (post NATE uhl)
posterity (poss TARE uh tee)   postpone (post PONE)
postgraduate (post GRAD yoo uht) postwar (POST WAR)
postlude (POST lude)

Roots	Suffixes
bell—war	al—relating to
lud—movement	ity—that which (those who)
mort—death	um—that which
nat—birth	

after

Postwar problems beset a nation _____ a war.

In American history the South before the Civil War is known as the antebellum South; the South immediately after the Civil War is known as the

postbellum

_____ South. Postwar and postbellum mean the same thing, but the latter term is used to distinguish a particular war. If you postpone something, you put it _____ something else.

after

your "after part," or bottom

If you sit on your posterior, you sit on what? _____

If you wish to make the world a better place for your posterity, you are concerned for your children, those

after

who come _____ you.

Prenatal care (before birth) of a baby is equally as

postnatal

important as _____ care. (after birth)

postgraduate

For those who wish a higher degree, undergraduate work at a college is followed by _____ work.

after death
post—after
mort—death

When the cause of death needs to be ascertained, a postmortem examination is made. <u>Postmortem</u> means _____.

postlude

If a <u>prelude</u> is a beginning musical piece or movement, a concluding musical piece or movement would be called a _____.

Self-Test

1. "Get off your _____; there's work to be done!" growled the sergeant. ("after parts"; bottoms)

2. In her novel Miss Poindexter gives a realistic description of conditions prevailing in the _____ South. (after the Civil War)

3. We owe it to our posterity to preserve as much of our natural environment as possible. Who are our <u>posterity</u>? _____ _____

4. A postmortem examination is required when the cause of death is not known. <u>Postmortem</u> means _____.

5. She knew the program was nearly over because the organist had struck up the _____. (concluding musical piece)

6. Darlene had many problems during her pregnancy, but fortunately there were no _____ complications. (after birth)

7. The university had acquired a fine reputation for the quality of its _____ _____ program. (after graduation)

Answers to Self-Test

1. posteriors 2. postbellum 3. those who come after us; our children
4. after death 5. postlude 6. postnatal 7. postgraduate

(15) PRE-, before

Derivatives:

precocious (pree KOHSH us)   preside (pree ZIDE)
prefix (PREE fix)   prestressed (PREE STRESSED)
premonition (prem un ISH un)   preview (PREE view)
presentiment (pree ZENT uh munt)

Roots	Suffixes
mon—warn	ion—act of
sent—feel	ious—characterized by being
sid—sit	ment—result of

A word part placed (fixed) before a root is a

prefix   _____.

A first showing of a play or movie before it is com-

preview   mercially available is a _____.

To prestress a building material is to introduce in-
ternal stress into it so that it will be able to withstand
loads applied to it later in a structure of some kind.
Today many buildings and other kinds of structures

prestressed   are made of _____ concrete.

The young mother had a presentiment that her child
was in trouble. If sent means "feeling," what is a

foreknowledge; an   presentiment? _____
intuitive feeling
before the fact   _____
is known

The person in charge of a group usually "sits before"
it, controlling the discussion or activities. That is,

presides   he _____.

At one time or other you have probably had a premonition of danger. If mon means "warning," what do

a "warning before-   you think premonition means? _____
hand," often coming
in a seemingly   _____
mysterious way   As you may have gathered, presentiment and premonition have almost identical meanings.

Although coc means "cook," the literal meaning of
precocious is not "precooked" but "cooked ahead of
time." In actual usage, a child that develops much

precocious   ahead of his age is said to be _____.

Self-Test

1. The supermarket manager had a _____
   that the roof was going to collapse. (feeling or warning before—two different words will fit here)

2. Like so many gifted composers, Mozart was a precocious child. What
   does <u>precocious</u> mean in this context? _____

   _____

3. Since the president was ill, he asked the vice-president to _____
   at the meeting. (sit before; take charge)

4. The new garage was put up in six days because it was made chiefly of prestressed concrete. <u>Prestressed</u> means _____

   _____.

Answers to Self-Test

1. premonition or presentiment 2. that he showed musical ability far in advance of his age 3. preside 4. subjected to stress before being built into a structure

(16)   PRO-, forward, in front of, in favor of

Derivatives:
proclivity (pro KLIV uh tee)   profuse (pro FEWSS)
procreate (PRO kree ate)   prolix (PRO lix)
profane (pro FANE)   propel (pro PELL)
profanity (pro FAN uh tee)   propose (pruh POSE)

<u>Roots</u>   <u>Suffixes</u>
cliv—lean   ity—quality of
create—bring forth
fane—shrine, church
fus—pour
lix—to be liquid
pel—push, urge

forward

The most common meaning of <u>pro-</u> is "forward." To
<u>propel</u> yourself into politics is to push _____,
to go into politics with a great deal of energy.

tendency

<u>Cliv</u> means "lean." To have a <u>proclivity</u> for drinking
means "act of leaning forward" and thus means: dislike of/tendency.

propose

The mayor will _____ a new transit system. ("put forward")

prolix

The mayor is a _____ speaker. (The words keep pouring forward like liquid.) Prolix means wordy.

Population could be controlled if people would pro-create less. What do you think procreate means?

to reproduce; to bring forth children

_____

When you give profuse thanks to a friend who has done

you repeat the thanks; "pour forth" more thanks than needed

you a favor, what do you do? _____

_____

worldly

Pro- can also mean "in front of." Profane language is literally language used "in front of (outside) a shrine or church." In other words, profane language is: religious/worldly. This same idea is carried out in the word profanity, meaning swearing or the use of crude language.

Occasionally pro- means "in favor of," as in pro-American or pro-unionism. If you take sides on some issue, in favor of the British, you are

pro-British

_____ .

Self-Test

1. Roger has a proclivity for getting into trouble with women. What does proclivity mean? _____

2. I certainly agree that Senator Phogbound is a prolix speaker. Prolix means _____ .

3. If human beings continue to _____ at this rate, the world population will double in thirty years. (bring forth children; re-produce)

4. Miss Durgess frowned and covered her ears; she was certain Mr. Putnam was going to use _____ language. (crude; full of swearing; not sacred)

5. He made profuse apologies for being so late. Profuse means _____

_____

Answers to Self-Test

1. tendency, inclination, bias 2. wordy; using more words than necessary
3. procreate 4. profane 5. "pouring forward"; doing more than really necessary; repeating the apologies

 SUB-, under, below

Derivatives:

subarctic (sub ARK tik)   subordinate (sub ORD in uht)
subconscious (sub KON shuss)   subterranean (sub ter AIN ee un)
subservient (sub SERVE ee unt)   succumb (suh KUM)
subside (sub SIDE)   suppress (suh PRESS)
subjugate (SUB jew gate)

Roots	Suffixes
cumb—burden	anean—characterized by being
jug—yoke	ent—characterized by being
ord—order, control	
sid—sit, settle	

under   A <u>subordinate</u> is a person _____ the influence or control of someone else, as in a job or the military. This relationship works best if there is mutual respect. However, if the person who serves under another is slavishly obedient and polite, like a

subservient   servant, then he is _____ servient (and he probably makes his superior feel contempt for him).

Hitler tried to subjugate all of Europe. <u>Subjugate</u>

under the yoke   translates into "put _____."
   sub—under
   jug—yoke

succumb   <u>Sub</u> + <u>cumb</u> turns into _____ because the <u>b</u> in <u>sub-</u> assimilates. In the sentence "Denise finally succumbed to the temptation," <u>suc-</u>

under   <u>cumb</u> means literally "to fall _____ a burden." In the sentence "He <u>succumbed</u> to pneumonia," succumb means "died."

When a storm <u>subsides</u>, it "settles under" (settles down). It's sad but true: passion is also known to

subside   _____.

Write down the derivative that matches the literal meaning:
subconscious   below consciousness = _____

subarctic   below the arctic = _____

subterranean   below the ground (terr) = _____

suppress   to press under = _____

Self-Test

1. Samantha showed her resentment in having to work for Mrs. Jones by behaving in a _____ manner. (slavishly obedient or
   polite)

2. When the excitement of the honeymoon had _____, they
   discovered they were not very compatible. (settled down)

3. Marsden succumbed to a heart attack. Succumb means _____

   _____.

4. Something that is below the surface of the ground is _____.

5. There are wild tribesmen living in these mountains who have never been
   subjugated. What does subjugated mean? _____

   _____.

6. Heading the committee will be John Mercedes and two of his subordinates.
   What are subordinates? _____

Answers to Self-Test

1. subservient 2. subsided 3. to die 4. subterranean 5. brought under the
yoke; dominated or tamed 6. people under the influence or control of somebody else

(18)   SUPER-, over

Derivatives:

superabundance (soo per uh BUN   superfluous (soo PERF loo us)
   dunce)   superlative (soo PERL uh tiv)
superannuated (soo per ANN yoo   supernumerary (soo per NOOM er
   ate uhd)   air ee)
supercharge (SOO per CHARGE)   supervisor (SOO per vize er)
superficial (soo per FISH uhl)

Roots	Suffixes
flu—flow	ary—one who
lat—carry	ate—verb ending
numer—number	ial—characterized by being
vis—see	ous—characterized by being

looks over super—over vis—look	A supervisor _____ the work of others.
superabundance	After two weeks of workouts, the boxer was super-charged with energy. He had a _____ abundance of energy.
over	Grandfather Bates's Model T Ford is superannuated. Literally that means _____ a year old, but the modern meaning is "out of date, too old for service." People who reach the age of 65 often find
superannuated	they are considered to be _____, too. (outdated) They are forced to retire.
	A superficial wound is not serious, since it occurs only on the surface of the body. A shallow remark about a subject, which shows an understanding only at the surface level, may also be called
superficial	_____.
"flowing over" super—over flu—flow	Any further discussion would be superfluous. Super-fluous translates into "_____" what is necessary or required.
extras	In the theatre supernumeraries are: extras/stars/clowns.
	Sometimes super is better defined as meaning "beyond." If you describe a meal, a performance, or the like in superlatives, you use the highest words of praise (you "carry beyond" the usual). Uncle Harry
superlatives	used _____ in describing Aunt Margaret's chocolate cake. Typical superlatives are adjectives such as "the best," "the finest," "the most fantastic."

Self-Test

1. This season Gerald got to see the operas free by working as a _____ _____. (extra)

2. Beware of movies advertised with _____ such as "the most sensational" or "the most expensive" ever made. (excessive words of praise)

3. When the balloon was losing height rapidly, we had to throw overboard

everything that was _____. (beyond what was really necessary; overflowing)

4. As machines take over more and more work, the people of the future may find themselves superannuated at the age of thirty-five. What does super- annuated mean? _____

5. His sister chided him for making such a superficial remark about religion. What does superficial mean? _____

6. If you are supercharged with enthusiasm, you have (little/a great deal) of enthusiasm.

Answers to Self-Test

1. supernumerary 2. superlatives 3. superfluous 4. too old for service; outdated 5. shallow; hitting only the surface 6. a great deal of

(19) TRANS-, across, through, beyond

Derivatives:

transatlantic (trans at LAN tik)
transcend (tran SEND)
transcribe (tran SKRIBE)
transfer (trans FER)
transgression (trans GRESH un)

transient (TRAN shunt)
transitory (TRAN suh tore ee)
translate (trans LATE)
transport (trans PORT)

Roots
fer, lat—carry
gress—step, go
it—go
scend—climb
scrib—write

Suffixes
ic—relating to
ent—one who
ion—act of
ory—marked by

across

The commonest meaning of trans- is "across": A transatlantic flight is made _____ the Atlantic Ocean.

carried across
trans—across
port—carry

When goods are transported, they are _____ _____ from one place to another.

transcribes
trans—across
scribes—writes

When a secretary "writes across" from a set of sym- bols to words, we say she _____ her dictation.

carries the meaning
across from one
language to another

A person who translates languages does what? _____ _____

transferred

Mr. Dobble was _____ from Duluth to St. Paul. ("carried across" from one place to another)

transgression
  trans—across
  gress—go, step

A person who steps across the line between good and bad commits a moral _____.

through

Another meaning of <u>trans-</u> is "through": A hotel for <u>transients</u> is a hotel for people who are passing _____ and not staying long.

that it passes by
very quickly
("goes through")

Poets and philosophers and older people are fond of saying that life itself is <u>transitory</u>. What do you think they mean? _____

beyond

Occasionally <u>trans-</u> means "beyond." Mr. Edwards transcended his own physical limitations. Here <u>transcended</u> means that he "climbed _____" them.

Self-Test

1. Reverend Dimmesdale prayed that God would forgive his moral _____ _____. (acts of "stepping across" the line from good to bad)

2. The happiness they shared was _____. (passing quickly; lasting only a brief time)

3. Aunt Alice decided to rent out a room or two; she placed a sign in her front window saying "Rooms for Transients." She hoped to rent to people who were _____.

4. In acquiring an education on his own and later becoming a famous writer, he showed that it was possible to transcend the limitations of both poverty and a miserable childhood. <u>Transcend</u> means _____ _____.

5. Although it took her a long time, Miss Forbes was able to _____ Miss DeVoto's shorthand notes. ("write across")

6. Charles Lindbergh made the first solo _____ flight. (across the Atlantic Ocean)

Answers to Self-Test

1. transgressions 2. transitory 3. passing through but not staying long
4. climb beyond; get free of 5. transcribe 6. transatlantic
  Now that you've studied Latin prefixes, a new look at page 156 might be fun.

CHAPTER SIX
Less Common Latin Roots

The roots in this chapter are called less important only because fewer words are derived from them. They do account for many useful words, however, and will repay careful study. The following units are structured very simply. Given the literal (and sometimes the current) meaning of the derivatives, you are to match them with the contexts they best seem to fit.

①   ANIM, spirit

Derivatives:
     animation (an uh MAY shun)—liveliness (state of having much spirit)
     magnanimous (mag NAN uh muss)—having a large (generous) spirit
     animosity (an uh MAHSS uh tee)—a spirited feeling of ill will or resentment

animosity   Doreen could not understand Frank's _____ toward her; she had done nothing to offend him.

                His donating the land for a new public park was a

magnanimous   _____ gesture.

animation   There was not enough _____ in her expression to make her look young and lively in the photograph.

animosity   Ronald is unaware that he expresses _____ towards strangers. (ill will)

②   BEL, BELL, war

Derivatives:
     antebellum (ant ee BELL um)—before the war (especially the Civil War)
     bellicose (BELL uh koss)—having a disposition to fight or to start a fight
     belligerent (buh LIJ er unt)—waging war; actively hostile in mood
     Note. Although the meanings of <u>bellicose</u> and <u>belligerent</u> overlap, <u>bellicose</u> refers more to attitude and <u>belligerent</u> to actual fighting.

belligerent

The Secretary General of the United Nations asked the _____ nations to declare a truce for thirty-six hours.

antebellum

Many Southern states have attempted to preserve the most impressive of the _____ mansions.

bellicose

Aunt Elizabeth is a bit grumpy at times, but Uncle Henry is by nature nearly always _____. (ready to start a fight)

bellicose or belligerent (both mean "warlike")

Norman's _____ statements increased the tension of the men in the prison stockade. (two words will fit here)

3 CID, CIS, cut, kill

Derivatives:
    fratricide (FRAT ruh side)—murder of one's brother
    genocide (JEN uh side)—murder of a race or large group of people
    incision (in CIZ shun)—act of cutting into; place cut into
    matricide (MAT ruh side)—murder of one's mother
    patricide (PAT ruh side)—murder of one's father

fratricide

Cain slew his brother Abel and thus committed ____

_____.

incision

Mattie was pleased with her neat _____ and liked to show it off to friends who came to visit her in the hospital.

genocide

For a time some militants regarded any attempt at birth-control in the ghetto as synonymous with

_____.

matricide

Electra despised her mother and eventually persuaded her brother to help her in committing _____

_____.

genocide

During the final stages of the Biafran rebellion, some European observers were referring to the mass starvation of Biafrans as _____.

patricide

George was so angry with his father that for a moment he had the urge to commit _____.

(4)   COGN, know, be acquainted

Derivatives:
  cognizant (COG nuh zunt)—knowing; being acquainted with something
  incognito (in cog NEE toe)—disguised; without being known
  precognition (pree cog NISH un)—act of knowing ahead of time

incognito   To avoid being pestered by fans, he traveled _____

_____.

cognizant   He was fully _____ of his duties
                           as a father.

cognizant   At that age I was scarcely _____
                           of my responsibilities toward my little brothers and
                           sisters.

                           Arigo showed psychic ability in several situations,
precognition   such as the _____ of his own
                           death.

(5)   DOC, DOCT, teach

Derivatives:
  docile (DAHSS uhl)—easily taught
  doctrine (DOK trin)—something taught; the body of principles accepted by
      believers in a philosophy or school
  indoctrinate (in DOK trin ate)—to teach a particular view or principle

                           Some of the younger Puritans gradually began to slip
doctrine   away from the religious _____ of
                           the elders.

                           The North Korean communists seldom made direct
indoctrinate   attempts to _____ American
                           prisoners-of-war.

docile   It may be as unfortunate for a child to be too _____

_____ as to be too rebellious.

                           The governess disliked the children's cousin; his in-
docile   fluence seemed to make them less and less _____

_____.

⑥ FLEX, FLECT, bend, twist

Derivatives:
  flexible (FLEKS uh buhl)—able to bend; able to adapt
  genuflect (JEN yoo flekt)—bend the knee, as in religious obedience or in
    a gesture of respect to royalty
  reflection (ree FLEK shun)—act of bending or twisting back; careful
    thinking; image

	Narcissus sat beside a clear pool admiring his own
reflection	_____ in the water.
genuflected	The priest _____ before leaving the altar.
	Seeing that he had startled her, the custodian apolo-
reflections	gized for having interrupted her _____.
flexible	My time schedule is entirely _____ this afternoon.

⑦ FRAG, FRACT, break

Derivatives:
  fractious (FRAK shuss)—unmanageable (breaking out in crossness)
  fragile (FRAJ uhl)—delicate (easily broken)
  infraction (in FRAK shun)—a violation (a break within)

	He was punished rather severely for a minor
infraction	_____ of the rules.
fragile	At best, freedom is a _____ pos-session, easily lost or destroyed. (delicate)
	The traffic officer said it would cost me five dollars
infraction	for each _____.
fractious	It was a very _____ young colt—a surprising fact in view of the docile behavior of the mare. (unmanageable)

⑧ GREG, flock

Derivatives:
  congregate (KON gruh gate)—flock together; assemble
  desegregation (dee seg ruh GAY shun)—abolishment of the practice of
    segregating blacks and whites, especially in housing and in public
    schools

Derivatives (continued):
    gregarious (gruh GARE ee us)—liking to be with others
    segregate (SEG ruh gate)—to put into separate groups

gregarious	He was the kind of Irishman we met repeatedly: he was good-natured, witty, and highly _____.
segregated	First, the four different kinds of rock were _____ and then each was analyzed for its mineral composition. (put into separate groups)
desegregation	Busing students to different neighborhoods is one method of school _____.
gregarious	It is not surprising that Martha became a social director on a cruise ship; she has always been a _____ person. (liking to be with others)
congregate	The neighborhood kids used to _____ in the vacant lot beside Charlie's house. (flock together)

9   LUC, light

Derivatives:
    elucidate (ee LOOSE uh date)—to make clear by explanation (to make light shine out)
    lucid (LOO sid)—easy to understand (clear, lighted)
    translucent (trans LOO sunt)—allowing light to shine through but not allowing objects to be distinguished

translucent	The bathroom windows were fitted with _____ glass.
elucidate	The doctor said my medical insurance is inadequate, but he did not _____ the point. (make clear by explanation)
translucent	The greenhouse consisted of an aluminum framework covered with some kind of _____ plastic film. (allowing light to shine through)
lucid	His explanation of the engineering difficulties they encountered was brief but _____. (clear)

(10) OMNI, all

Derivatives:

omnipotent (ahm NIP uh tunt)—all-powerful
omniscient (ahm NISH unt)—all-knowing
omnivorous (ahm NIV er us)—eating both plant and animal substances
(eating all)

omnipotent

One expects a god to be _____.
(all-powerful)

"How should I know what will happen? After all, I

omniscient

am not _____."

A little boy that age sometimes thinks his father is

omnipotent

_____ and can do almost anything.

omnivorous

Man is an _____ creature enjoy-
ing a wide range of choices for his dinner table.

Self-Test

From the list at the right select the word that best fits each of the following contexts. No word is used twice, and there is one extra word.

1. The king was safe in the crowd as long as he

    remained _____. (disguised)

2. The yard supervisor broke up the fight and ordered the men to make peace with each other,

    but both remained _____.
    (actively hostile)

3. In his haste to leave, Father Murray almost

    forgot to _____ in front of the
    altar.

4. I felt his _____ reaching out
   to me from the letter. (ill will)

5. Miss Augustine looked at us as though our

    smiling and laughing were an _____
    of her private code. (violation)

6. Old prospectors like Scotty are not _____,
   and on first acquaintance they may even seem
   antisocial. (liking to be with others)

animosity
magnanimous
elucidate
gregarious
omnipotent
infraction
incognito
belligerent
indoctrinate
genuflect
fratricide

7. Apart from saying he was going to resign, John
    did not _____ his role in the
    controversy.

8. You should ask your father for your allowance now
    while he is being so _____.
    (generous)

9. Several generations of people were _____
    in the idea that might makes right.   (taught a belief)

10. The native god did not answer Tawita's prayer, but
    Tawita was not dismayed. Native gods were not ex-
    pected to be either reliable or _____.
    (all-powerful)

Answers to Self-Test

1. incognito 2. belligerent 3. genuflect 4. animosity 5. infraction 6. gregarious 7. elucidate 8. magnanimous 9. indoctrinated 10. omnipotent

(11)   REG, RIG, RECT, rule, straight, right

Derivatives:
    incorrigible (in KORE ij uh buhl)—unable to be ruled or controlled
    rectify (REK tuh feye)—straighten; make right
    rectitude (REK tuh tude)—upright character or conduct; honesty
    regimen (REJ uh mun)—rule; systematic course of therapy or treatment

regimen   The dietary _____ prescribed by the
                   doctor limited him to 600 calories a day.

rectify   She tried very hard to _____ her
                   mistakes. (make right)

                   I like Barney, too, but I must admit that he is an
incorrigible   _____ liar. (uncontrollable)

                   Betty will not babysit for the Joneses any more; she
incorrigible   says their three children are _____.

                   The more Reverend Dimmesdale declared his own
                   sin and weakness, the more he convinced his congre-
rectitude   gation of his moral _____. (upright
                   character)

(12) SEQU, SECUT, follow

Derivatives:

inconsequential (in kon suh KWEN shuhl)—not having important results following

persecute (PER suh kute)—to torment or punish (to follow thoroughly)

sequel (SEE kwuhl)—that which follows, as the next installment of a literary work

sequential (sih KWEN shuhl)—connected in a series (following)

persecuted

The Mormons were _____ before they migrated to Utah and founded their own religious colony. (tormented)

The side effects of taking this medicine are

inconsequential

_____ when compared to the good it does.

sequel

The _____ was called "Return to Peyton Place." (following work)

The catalogue numbers did not appear to be

sequential

_____.

The loss of twenty-five cents and ten minutes of my

inconsequential

time is _____.

(13) SON, sound

Derivatives:

dissonance (DISS uh nunce)—a combination of sounds that are unpleasant or unharmonious

resonance (REZ uh nunce)—quality of sounding back (echoing)

unison (YOO nuh sun)—sounding as one (one sound)

dissonance

Modern composers no longer avoid _____ in their works, and some even emphasize it. (unharmonious sounds)

unison

The children repeated the poem in _____. (as one)

resonance

There was enough _____ in Mr. Talman's voice that he could be heard without a microphone.

The box placed below the strings of a violin picks up

resonance

the sound from the strings and gives it _____

_____.

(14) STRING, STRICT, bind tight

Derivatives:

astringent (uh STRIN junt)—causing shrinking and contraction (binding
tight toward)

constrict (kun STRIKT)—draw together (bind tight with); compress

stringent (STRIN junt)—severe (binding tight)

constricted   His breathing was _____ by the
tight collar.

astringent   After shaving, he used an _____
lotion to firm up the skin and erase wrinkles.

Representatives from student organizations protested

stringent   the Dean's _____ new regulations.
(severe)

stringent   It may require very _____ measures
to curb inflation.

(15) TANG, TING, TACT, TIG, touch

Derivatives:

contingent (kun TIN junt)—depending on something uncertain (touching with)

contiguous (kun TIG yoo us)—in actual contact (touching together)

intact (in TAKT)—whole (not touched)

intangible (in TAN juh buhl)—without a physical basis (not able to be
touched)

tangible (TAN juh buhl)—real; having a physical basis (able to be touched)

intact   Few houses were left _____ after the
earthquake.

tangible   The judge asked whether there was _____
proof that a crime had been committed. (having a
physical basis)

Our plans for having a picnic tomorrow are

contingent   _____ on the weather.

contiguous   The two building sites are _____.
(in actual contact)

contingent   Building the new house is _____ on
being able to sell the old one.

In bargaining to buy Fred's grocery store, Mr. Mer-
dis said he would not pay a penny to purchase anything

intangible   as _____ as good will. (not able to be touched)

16   TEN, TIN, TAIN, hold

Derivatives:
> incontinence (in KON tuh nunce)—lack of self-control (lack of holding together)
> tenacious (ten AY shus)—persistent (holding on)
> tenure (TEN yer)—possession; length of time of holding or possessing
> untenable (un TEN uh buhl)—incapable of being held or defended

tenure   On April 15 Ruby will have twenty years of _____ in this office.

incontinence   We were all offended by the _____ of his language.

      The desertion of his financial supporters left him in

untenable   an _____ position. (indefensible)

      With his partner's continual complaining and competitiveness, their partnership finally became

untenable   _____.

tenacious   He was a _____ old man and kept working his claim for weeks after all the other miners had left the mountain.

17   TEND, TENS, TENT, stretch

Derivatives:
> contentious (kun TEN shus)—quarrelsome (stretching with)
> distend (diss TEND)—to stretch apart; over-fill
> extensive (eks TEN siv)—broad; affecting many things (stretched out)

distended   His stomach was _____ by all the extra food he had eaten.

extensive   The research had covered an extremely _____ field. (wide)

      Lawton did not like working with Belvedere because

contentious   Belvedere was _____. (argumentative)

contentious

At the time of their first encounter Mr. Jericho
sized up the mayor as being insecure and _____
_____.

(18)   TENU, thin

Derivatives:
   attenuate (uh TEN yoo ate)—weaken; lessen in force (make thinner)
   extenuate (eks TEN yoo ate)—lessen the seriousness of something by
      making excuses (thin out)
   tenuous (TEN yoo us)—insubstantial (thin)

tenuous

The patient had a very _____ hold on
reality. (thin; insubstantial)

extenuating

A criminal often pleads _____
circumstances to justify his actions. (excusing; les-
sening seriousness)

attenuated

The agency was reorganized and left with greatly
_____ responsibility for
child care and guidance. (weakened)

tenuous

Ruth's arguments were _____ and
unconvincing. (insubstantial)

(19)   TRACT, draw, pull

Derivatives:
   distract (diss TRAKT)—draw away attention (draw apart)
   intractable (in TRAKT uh buhl)—stubborn (unable to be pulled or led)
   traction (TRAK shun)—a drawing or pulling

intractable

General de Gaulle had a reputation for being an
_____ politician. (stubborn)

traction

While the pain persists in the lower back, he will
have to remain in _____. (a
drawing or pulling)

traction

The accident occurred because the car could not
maintain proper _____ on the
muddy highway.

distract

None of us could _____ him long
enough for Julie to hide the package.

VER, true

Derivatives:

veracity (ver ASS suh tee)—truthfulness

verisimilitude (veer uh suh MILL uh tude)—an appearance of truth or reality (similarity to the truth)

verity (VARE uh tee)—truth; true statement

veracity

Mildred said indignantly that no one had ever before questioned her _____. (truthfulness)

verisimilitude

The use of a documentary technique helped to give the movie greater _____.

veracity

It never occurred to Mrs. Littlejohn to doubt the fellow's _____.

verities

Old Man Perkins lectured away at us, confident that he was in touch with the eternal _____. (truths)

Self-Test

From the list at the right select the word that best fits each of the following contexts. No word is used twice, and there is one extra word.

1. Professor Potter winced at the _____ caused when I hit the wrong keys.

2. Kevin soon regretted the _____ of his language.

3. He needed physical exercise. The _____ prescribed for him included jogging, swimming, and bicycling.

4. Something in human nature resists regulations that are too _____.

5. The Bishop admitted there might be _____ _____ factors in Lady Margery's case but was not inclined to be lenient toward her.

6. A playwright can take liberties with plot, dialogue, and characterization as long as he somehow manages to achieve _____.

7. The four of us pleaded with him to change his mind,

inconsequential
contentious
contiguous
dissonance
incontinence
extenuating
regimen
verisimilitude
intractable
stringent
tangible

but Matthew remained _____.
(stubborn)

8. Washington and Oregon are _____
    states. (their borders touch)

9. Moody, egotistical, and _____,
    he was avoided by all the other apprentices.
    (quarrelsome)

10. The manager dismissed the matter of repairs,

    saying it was _____.

Answers to Self-Test

1. dissonance 2. incontinence 3. regimen 4. stringent 5. extenuating
6. verisimilitude 7. intractable 8. contiguous 9. contentious 10. inconsequential

   Now that you've mastered this chapter, you might enjoy a new look at
the drawing that opens it on page 188.

SEPTIFEATHERED

HEPTAFEATHERED

CHAPTER SEVEN
Greek and Latin Numerals

English	Greek	Latin
one	mono	uni
two	di	du
three	tri	tri
four	tetra	quadr
five	penta	quint
six	hexa	sex
seven	hepta	sept
eight	oct	oct
nine	ennea	nov
ten	dec	dec
hundred	hecto	cent
thousand	kilo	mill

Very few English words are derived from the Greek root _ennea_, and even these are infrequently used: _Ennead_, _enneagon_. Similarly, only a few common words are derived from the Latin root _nov_: _November_ (the ninth month in the old Roman calendar), _novena_ (in the Roman Catholic church, saying prayers or holding services on nine days).

In the metric system, the Greek root _deca_ is used to mean ten: _decade_ (ten years). The Latin root _deci_ is used to mean one tenth (1/10): _decimal_, _decimate_ (kill one in ten). The Greek root _hecto_ means one hundred: _hecto-liter_ (100 liters); the Latin root _centi_ also means one hundred but is commonly used to mean one hundredth (1/100): _centiliter_ (one hundredth of a liter). The Greek root _kilo_ means one thousand: _kilometer_ (one thousand meters); the Latin root _milli_ means one thousandth (1/1000): _millimeter_ (one thousandth of a meter).

Self-Test

1. If you speak in one tone of voice, you speak in a: bitone/monotone.

2. How many babies are born at the same time if there are _quintuplets_?

   _____

3. A figure or area with four angles is a: quadrangle/triangle.

4. A famous five-sided building in Washington, D.C., is called the: Pentagon/Octagon.

5. An athlete who can compete in ten different sports events enters what contest in the Olympic games? (the hexapod/the decathlon)

6. How many instrumentalists are featured in an octet? _____

7. A state with a unicameral legislative system has: two legislative bodies/one legislative body.

8. A person in his seventies is called a: sexagenarian/septuagenarian.

9. In the metric system one hundred grams would make up a unit called a: hectogram/milligram.

10. A milliliter of water would be: one thousand liters/one thousandth of a liter.

11. The Ten Commandments can also be called the: Eulogy/Decalog.

12. Richard estimates we will have to drive another fifteen _____ meters to reach Paris. (use the Greek root for thousand)

13. If you speak four languages, you are _____ilingual. (use the Latin root)

14. The specimen was trisected. It was cut into how many parts? _____

15. This creature is the only one of its kind. It is therefore _____que. (use the Latin root)

16. A worm-like creature that seems to have a hundred feet is a _____ipede. (use the Latin root for hundred)

17. A period of one thousand years is a _____ennium. (use the Latin root)

18. An athlete who wishes to compete in only five different sports events enters what contest in the Olympic games? (the pentathlon/the enneathlon)

19. A century is a period of how many years? _____

20. A fair celebrating the one hundredth birthday of something is a: (centennial/perennial) affair.

Answers to Self-Test

1. monotone 2. five 3. quadrangle 4. Pentagon 5. decathlon 6. eight
7. one legislative body 8. septuagenarian 9. hectogram 10. one thousandth
of a liter 11. Decalog 12. kilometers 13. quadrilingual 14. three 15. unique
16. centipede 27. millenium 18. the pentathlon 19. one hundred years
20. centennial

If you missed it the first time around, your new knowledge of Greek and Latin numerals should now unlock the fowl mystery on page 202.

Final Self-Test

In the blank at the left of each question, write the number of the definition that best fits the meaning of the word underlined. Most of the words were specifically covered in the book; some were not, but are made up of word parts studied. In either case, use your knowledge of word parts to help you choose the best answer, according to the literal meaning of the word. (If you plan to take this test before reading the book and again afterward, be sure to write your answers on a separate sheet of paper, not in the book.) Answers are given following the Self-Test.

_____ 1. Hank hit an <u>unprecedented</u> number of home runs.
(1) without an earlier model or pattern
(2) clear and uncomplicated
(3) without reasoning or planning to

_____ 2. Mr. Ormsby is the chief <u>malefactor</u> in this story about nineteenth-century millionaires.
(1) leader
(2) mill-owner
(3) evil-doer

_____ 3. The president said the pact with the European countries would be <u>conducive</u> to world peace.
(1) opposed to
(2) leading to
(3) not relating to

_____ 4. The Joneses were soon bogged down in expensive <u>litigation</u>.
(1) remodeling
(2) intensive medical care
(3) lawsuit

_____ 5. John was unexpectedly overcome by a feeling of <u>claustrophobia</u>.
(1) fear of water
(2) fear of high places
(3) fear of being shut in

_____ 6. A <u>malevolent</u> expression would indicate:
(1) good will
(2) illness
(3) evil intent

_____ 7. A <u>cursory</u> reading of a book would be:
  (1) extremely careful
  (2) very pleasurable
  (3) a hasty running through

_____ 8. Tim is <u>credulous</u>.
  (1) too readily believing
  (2) dull or stupid
  (3) easygoing

_____ 9. Mr. Beamis is a <u>recluse</u>.
  (1) one who loves animals of all kinds.
  (2) one who loves only money
  (3) one who shuts himself away from society

_____ 10. To <u>recapitulate</u> a lecture is to:
  (1) make a summary
  (2) take something apart
  (3) change the original meaning

_____ 11. Government statistics showed a <u>per capita</u> expense of $4,000.
  (1) by or for the government
  (2) by or for each person
  (3) an amount left after deductions

_____ 12. Our instructions were quite <u>explicit</u>.
  (1) given by someone in authority
  (2) clearly stated
  (3) without detail

_____ 13. Miss Hopkins called attention to Roger's <u>deferential</u> manner of treating her.
  (1) showing dislike
  (2) showing ignorance about something
  (3) showing respect

_____ 14. To be accused of <u>duplicity</u> is to be accused of:
  (1) spiteful actions
  (2) double-dealing
  (3) insincere efforts to please

_____ 15. The patient's behavior is <u>regressive</u>.
  (1) going back to an earlier level
  (2) moody and changeable
  (3) lacking control

_____ 16. The equipment used in this kind of construction is very <u>ponderous</u>.
  (1) heavy and unwieldy
  (2) old-fashioned and unsuitable
  (3) quite expensive

17. I was soon aware of an <u>incongruity</u> between his words and his actions.
    (1) lack of agreement
    (2) agreement
    (3) missing connection

18. The reporter questioned the <u>efficacy</u> of such cold remedies.
    (1) hidden danger
    (2) side effect
    (3) ability to carry out its intended function

19. The gift brought on a feeling of <u>elation</u>.
    (1) disappointment
    (2) reward for services rendered
    (3) joy or pride

20. By the time he was thirty-three, he was a <u>facile</u> writer.
    (1) able to write with ease
    (2) given to serious discussions
    (3) having great merit

21. The construction of the bridge was a <u>superlative</u> engineering accomplishment.
    (1) requiring the cooperation of many people
    (2) carried to the highest level
    (3) seeming to require divine or non-human help

22. The Smith children were <u>incorrigible</u> last Saturday evening.
    (1) not easily discouraged
    (2) having physical ills of some kind
    (3) unmanageable or uncontrollable

23. His anger was expressed in an <u>incontinent</u> flow of words.
    (1) not logical; emotional
    (2) not entirely clear and connected
    (3) not held back or controlled

24. Until he was eighteen he had never done any <u>introspective</u> thinking.
    (1) imaginary
    (2) unlimited
    (3) looking within

25. The <u>sentimentality</u> of the poem appealed to him.
    (1) exaggerated tender feeling
    (2) characteristics of old age
    (3) guilty feeling

26. A <u>sedentary</u> occupation:
    (1) involves a great deal of sitting
    (2) centers on an important area of work
    (3) supports a more important job

27. To have the <u>stamina</u> of a long-distance runner is to have:
    (1) a special body rhythm
    (2) expert physical coordination
    (3) endurance

28. If you have a <u>presentiment</u> of danger, you have:
    (1) foreknowledge
    (2) an unjustified opinion
    (3) a slight indication

29. <u>Diaphanous</u> material allows something to:
    (1) be seen through it
    (2) be attached to it
    (3) be attracted to it

30. What does an <u>astringent</u> lotion do?
    (1) It binds the skin tight.
    (2) It loosens the skin.
    (3) It makes a person look younger.

31. Sylvia refused to participate in any <u>occult</u> ceremonies.
    (1) mysterious; based on hidden knowledge
    (2) unprepared or unrehearsed
    (3) costly or time-consuming

32. At that time Venice was an <u>affluent</u> society.
    (1) living on or near water
    (2) shifting locations periodically
    (3) having an abundance of wealth for most members

33. To <u>abjure</u> dishonesty in politics is to:
    (1) swear oneself as being opposed to dishonesty in politics
    (2) swear to the existence of dishonesty in politics
    (3) be upset by dishonesty in politics

34. The first explorers were surprised to discover these natives worshipping <u>anthropomorphic</u> gods.
    (1) cruel to human beings
    (2) having both sexes in one being
    (3) having human characteristics

35. The author called Senator Hargis a clever <u>demagogue</u>.
    (1) public speaker
    (2) unimportant official
    (3) one who leads the people by appealing to their worst nature

36. An <u>autonomous</u> state is:
    (1) self-ruling
    (2) just coming into being politically
    (3) dominated by machines and industry

_____ 37. A <u>eulogy</u> is a speech in which someone is:
   (1) belittled
   (2) praised
   (3) welcomed

_____ 38. A great deal of publicity was given to his <u>eccentricities</u>.
   (1) illegitimate children
   (2) illegal actions
   (3) unconventional actions

_____ 39. In <u>retrospect</u> I see that my problems were really minor.
   (1) looking backward
   (2) seeing from all angles
   (3) admitting error

_____ 40. <u>Hyperactive</u> children are:
   (1) underactive
   (2) overactive
   (3) troublesome to deal with

_____ 41. The humor in the movie is based on <u>anachronisms</u>.
   (1) predictions about the future
   (2) incidents taken from the past
   (3) errors in time

_____ 42. A <u>panacea</u> for the world's ills would be a:
   (1) forced action
   (2) one-sided solution
   (3) cure-all

_____ 43. A <u>heterogenous</u> group of people would contain people:
   (1) unable to reproduce
   (2) having similar characteristics
   (3) having different characteristics

_____ 44. How many people does it take to form a <u>sextet</u>?
   (1) two
   (2) six
   (3) seven

_____ 45. If something is two <u>millimeters</u> wide, it is:
   (1) two thousand meters wide
   (2) two-thousandths of a meter wide

_____ 46. Miss Darnell <u>acceded</u> to our request.
   (1) yielded
   (2) denied
   (3) considered fully

_____ 47. The <u>diffusion</u> of his energies left him incapable of finishing all his projects on time.
   (1) decline
   (2) rapid use
   (3) being scattered over a large area

____ 48. He referred to his mistress <u>euphemistically</u> as his "social secretary."
  (1) in a manner marked by the lack of any emotion
  (2) in a manner marked by emotional overtones
  (3) in a manner marked by using pleasant-sounding rather than harsh or realistic words

____ 49. An <u>omnivorous</u> creature:
  (1) hunts only at night
  (2) eats both plant and animal substances
  (3) has no enemies more powerful than itself

____ 50. In the fairy tale a witch is said to be fond of <u>metamorphosing</u> small children.
  (1) leading small children astray
  (2) making accidents happen to small children
  (3) changing the form of small children

Answers to Final Self-Test

1. (1) without an earlier model or pattern ("without something having gone before")
2. (3) evil-doer ("one who does evil or bad")
3. (2) leading to ("marked by leading together")
4. (3) lawsuit ("act of carrying on a lawsuit")
5. (3) fear of being shut in ("fear of closed places")
6. (3) evil intent ("marked by bad will")
7. (3) a hasty running through ("marked by running")
8. (1) too readily believing ("marked by believing")
9. (3) one who shuts himself away from society ("one shut back")
10. (1) make a summary ("carry to a head again")
11. (2) by or for each person ("per head")
12. (2) clearly stated ("folded out"; unfolded)
13. (3) showing respect ("marked by carrying down" one's own importance)
14. (2) double-dealing ("state of two folds")
15. (1) going back to an earlier level ("marked by stepping backward")
16. (1) heavy and unwieldy ("characterized by weight")
17. (1) lack of agreement ("state of not coming together")
18. (3) ability to carry out its intended function ("quality of making out")
19. (3) joy or pride ("state of being carried outside" oneself)
20. (1) able to write with ease ("able to do or make")
21. (2) carried to the highest level ("characterized by being carried above")
22. (3) unmanageable or uncontrollable ("not able to be ruled, not able to be made straight")
23. (3) not held back or controlled ("marked by being not held together")
24. (3) looking within ("characterized by looking inside")
25. (1) exaggerated tender feeling ("state of feeling")
26. (1) involves a great deal of sitting ("characterized by sitting")

27. (3) endurance ("ability to stand"—that is, to keep on one's feet)
28. (1) foreknowledge ("a feeling beforehand")
29. (1) be seen through it ("characterized by being clear throughout")
30. (1) It binds the skin tight. (astringent = "that which binds toward")
31. (1) mysterious; based on hidden knowledge ("marked by being covered up"—that is, hidden)
32. (3) having an abundance of wealth for most members ("characterized by flowing toward")
33. (1) swear oneself as being opposed to dishonesty in politics ("to swear away")
34. (3) having human characteristics ("having the shape of man")
35. (3) one who leads the people by appealing to their worst nature ("people leader")
36. (1) self-ruling ("characterized by self-rule")
37. (2) praised ("good speech, " "act of saying good things")
38. (3) unconventional actions ("acts that are off-center")
39. (1) looking backward ("backward look")
40. (2) overactive ("marked by being excessively active")
41. (3) errors in time ("things that are opposed in time"—that is, not of the same time order)
42. (3) cure-all ("that which cures everything")
43. (3) having different characteristics ("characterized by being of different kinds")
44. (2) six ("that which is composed of six" people)
45. (2) two-thousandths of a meter wide (millimeter = "a thousandth of a meter")
46. (1) yielded ("yielded to")
47. (3) being scattered over a large area ("act of pouring apart")
48. (3) in a manner marked by using pleasant-sounding rather than harsh or realistic words ("in a manner based on pleasant statements")
49. (2) eats both plant and animal substances ("characterized by eating everything")
50. (3) changing the form of small children ("current act of changing the form")

Appendix

The prefixes and roots used in this program.

PREFIXES	MEANING	EXAMPLES
Greek:		
a, an	without	adamant, amoral, atheism
anti, ant	against	antibiotic, antisocial, antagonist
cata	down	catapult, cataclysmic, catalyst
dia	across, through, thoroughly	diaphanous, diagonal, diathermy
epi	on, upon	epidermis, epitaph, epitomize
eu	good, pleasant	eugenics, eyphony, euthanasia
ec	out, outside	eccentric, ecstasy, mastectomy
hyper	over, excessive	hypercritical, hyperbole, hypersensitive
hypo	under, less than	hypoactive, hypodermic, hypothesis
para, par	alongside	parallel, paraphrase, parody
peri	around, near	perigee, periphery, periscope
syn, sym, syl, sys	together, with	syllable, symposium, syntax, system
Latin:		
ab, abs	from, away	aberrant, abrade, abstinence
ad (af, ag, al, am, an, ar, as)	to, toward	adore, aggravate, allocate, attract
ante	before	antedate, antediluvian, anteroom
circum	around	circumference, circumvent, circumspect
com, con, col, co	with, together	commingle, congruent, conjugal, co-operate

PREFIXES	MEANING	EXAMPLES
Latin:		
counter, contra, contro	against, opposite	countermand, contraband, controversy
de	down, away	decelerate, depose, descend
dis, dif, di	apart, not	discomfiture, diffident, digress
ex, ef, e	out	exempt, efface, eject
inter	between	intermittent, interregnum, interstate
intra, intro	within	intrastate, intravenous, introvert
ob, oc, of, op	against	obtuse, occult, offend, oppose
per	through, thoroughly	percolate, permeate, perspicacity
post	after	posterior, postlude, postnatal
pre	before	precocious, presentiment, preside
pro	forward, in front of, in favor of	procreate, prolix, pro-American
sub	under, below	subarctic, subjugate, subterranean
super	over	superannuated, superficial, superfluous
trans	across, through, beyond	transcend, transient, transitory

ROOTS	MEANING	EXAMPLES
Greek:		
anthrop, anthropo	man, mankind	anthropoid, misanthrope, philanthropy
arch	first, ancient, chief	archaic, archeology, oligarchy
chron	time	chronic, chronology, synchronize
dem, demo	people	demagogue, demographer, epidemic
dox	belief, teaching, opinion	doxology, orthodox, paradoxically
dyna	power	dynamics, dynasty, thermodynamics
gam	marriage	bigamy, misogamist, polygamy
gen	birth, race, kind	congenital, genealogy, progenitor
hydr	water	hydraulic, hydrophyte, hydroponics

ROOTS	MEANING	EXAMPLES
Greek:		
log, logy	speech, study of, collection of	astrology, monologue, zoology
mega, megalo	great	megalopolis, megaton, megavitamin
micro	small	microbe, microcosm, microorganism
morph	form	amorphous, metamorphosis, polymorphic
neo	new	neoclassical, neolithic, neophyte
nom	rule, law, systematized knowledge	agronomist, autonomous, metronome
onym	name	acronym, anonymously, pseudonym
pan	all	panacea, pandemonium, pantheon
path	feeling, suffering, disease	apathy, pathetic, psychopath
phil	love	Anglophile, philanderer, philter
pod, ped	foot	podiatrist, centipede, tripod
ped	child	pediatrician, pedagogue, pedagogy
poly	many	polyandry, Polynesia, polysyllabic
polit, polis	city, citizen	cosmopolitan, Indianapolis, politician
proto	first, fundamental	protocol, protoplasm, protozoa
pyr	fire	pyre, pyromania, pyrophobia
scop	see	horoscope, periscope, telescope
the	god	apotheosis, polytheism, theocracy
Latin:		
act, ag, ig,	do, drive, carry on, move	activate, agitate, agility
am, amat	love, loving	amateur, amiable, amorous
anim	spirit	animation, magnanimous, animosity
aqu	water	aqualung, aquatic, subaqueous
bel, bell	war	bellicose, belligerent, antebellum
bene	good	benefaction, benevolent, benign

ROOTS	MEANING	EXAMPLES
Latin:		
capt(t), cept, cip, ceiv, ceit	seize, take	captivate, perception, recipient, deceive, conceit
capit	head	capitol, decapitate, per capita
carn	flesh	carnage, carnivore, reincarnation
cede, ceed, cess	go, move, yield	accede, proceed, recession
cid, cis	cut, kill	fratricide, incision, genocide
clam, claim	cry, shout	clamor, disclaim, reclamation
cogn	know, be acquainted	cognizant, incognito, precognition
clud, clus, clois claus	shut, close	exclude, inclusion, cloister, claustrophobia
corp	body	corporeal, corpuscle, incorporate
cred	believe	credence, incredible, credulous
cur, cour	run	cursory, incursion, courier
dict	say, speak, tell	dictator, jurisdiction, valedictorian
doc, doct	teach	docile, doctrine, indoctrinate
duct, duc	lead	aqueduct, seduce, seductive
fac, fact, fect, fic, feat, feas, fy	do, make	facile, factory, perfectionist, proficient, feasible, magnify
fer, lat	bear, carry	conifer, differentiate, relate
fid	faith	confidant, fidelity, perfidious
flex, flect	bend, twist	flexible, genuflect, reflection
frag, fract	break	fractious, fragile, infraction
fus, fund, found	pour	effusive, refund, foundry
grad, gress	step, go	aggressive, degrade, digress
jac, ject	throw, hurl	conjecture, ejaculation, eject
luc	light	elucidate, lucid, translucent
mal	bad	malady, malevolent, malodorous
mit, miss	send	transmit, remittance, remission
omni	all	omnipotent, omniscient, omnivorous
pens, pend, pond	hang, weigh	appendage, dispense, ponderous

ROOTS	MEANING	EXAMPLES
Latin:		
plic, pli, ply	fold, bend	complication, imply, pliant
reg, rig, rect	rule, straight, right	incorrigible, rectify, regimen
scrib, script	write	ascribe, conscription, nondescript
sed, sid, sess	sit	sedentary, assiduous, session
sent, sens	feel	dissent, sentiment, sensuous
sequ, secut	follow	inconsequential, persecute, sequel
solv, solut	free, loosen	absolution, resolve, solvent
son	sound	dissonance, resonance, unison
spec, spic	look	perspective, retrospect, conspicuous
spir	breathe	aspire, expire, spirometer
string, strict	bind tight	astringent, constrict, stringent
tang, ting, tact, tig	touch	tangible, contingent, intact, contiguous
tempor	time	contemporary, tempo, temporize
ten, tin, tain	hold	tenacious, incontinence, retain
tend, tens, tent	stretch	distend, extensive, contentious
tenu	thin	attenuate, extenuate, tenuous
tort	twist	contortion, retort, tortuous
tract	draw, pull	distract, intractable, traction
ver	true	veracity, verisimilitude, verity
vid, vis	see, look	invidious, providence, supervise
voc, vocat, vok	call, calling	advocate, convocation, invoke, vocal

Index